WHITE HOT GRIEF PARADE

ALSO BY ALEXANDRA SILBER

After Anatevka

WHITE HOT GRIEF PARADE

A MEMOIR

ALEXANDRA SILBER

PEGASUS BOOKS
NEW YORK LONDON

WHITE HOT GRIEF PARADE

Pegasus Books Ltd.
148 West 37th Street, 13th FL
New York, NY 10018

First Pegasus Books cloth edition July 2018

Interior design by Sabrina Plomitallo-González

ISBN: 978-1-68177-764-1

10 9 8 7 6 5 4 3 2 1

Printed in the United States of America
Distributed by W. W. Norton & Company, Inc.

TABLE OF CONTENTS

PART ONE
DEATH

Things I'd Tell My Seventeen-Year-Old Self

Whenever I meet people, they inevitably get curious about the idiosyncratic arc of my life. Common questions include: *"Where did you go to college?"* or *"How did you end up in the UK?"* The answers, of course, are complicated, because in the autumn of 2001, I lost my father to a lifelong battle with cancer. I was just eighteen, only a few months out of high school, and a few weeks into my freshman year of college.

What followed was a very strange and challenging chapter of my life that I rarely take out and examine, for obvious reasons.

Thus, I do what we all do: I "CliffsNotes" it—that is, I give you the *gist*. I skip over this bizarre chapter of *Twilight Zone* weirdness that for many years I felt no one else could possibly understand (unless they were, by some coincidence, *there*). So whenever I tell the "CliffsNotes story of my life" it goes like this:

My dad died.
I moved to Scotland.
I grew up.
And here we are at this cocktail party.

But of course, everyone's story is more nuanced than that. For all of us there exists that space between the lines of our first two CliffsNotes sentences—the space where a universe of life occurred. Where I faced, experienced, and walked within the universal fear all humanity—regardless of time period, culture or status—spends its waking hours fending off: the loss of someone they love. Where, like so many others who overcome adversity, I learned to *stand back up*. At the intersection of childhood and adulthood.

At eighteen, I suppose no one would have blamed me for capitulating to grief under such circumstances. It was a mighty blow at such a crucial moment in anyone's development. Despite being bright, hardworking, and full of ambitions, I was also sensitive and did not have the appropriate skills to cope with such a loss.

Yet, in reflection I recognize that the secret of my personal resilience lay within that enigmatic fold between those CliffsNotes lines, lessons gifted to me by the people who shared the chapter—in every way the heroes of this story and of my actual life—who lifted, taught, and revealed to me what I am—what we all are—truly made of. It was in the "in-between" chapter that I experienced the thing every human being fears the most, and I lived. And, having lived, I learned; What else was there to be afraid of? The loss provided the ultimate gift: fearlessness.

Some people tell me I was brave. But I didn't *feel* brave. I felt terrified. It was in this secret chapter that I learned one can't be courageous unless one feels afraid. I felt compelled to write the invisible chapter down and own every messy, awkward, ugly, hilarious, roaring, agonizing moment. To document standing back up.

I know now that such a document doesn't begin with the death. It begins right now—looking back upon those charmed and sacred days, the moments before it all came crashing down.

( )

Before we lost Dad, before the dying and the feuding and the grieving, there was just me: Al, a seventeen-year-old with her own set of concerns and everything ahead of her.

Here's what I'd tell my seventeen-year-old self:

1. It is all ahead of you.

2. You are not fat.

3. That thing you are all working so hard to prevent? It is going to happen. Soon. Enjoy this last year. Go on a lot of walks with your dad, ask for more stories, remember his eyes, his smell, the squeeze of his hand. What seems like always and forever will be gone.

4. Frizz Ease. Buy it.

5. You're going to get many, many letters, phone calls, and all forms of messages from people about how much you and your entire family mean to them.

6. Some people are going to call you Alex rather than Al. Try to forgive; they know not what they do.

7. Wear sunscreen. All. The. Time.

8. Wear any outfit you want. Because you can.

9. You are not going to believe this, but you do not know everything. Also, your parents are right. About a lot of things.

10. There is life after not doing it all "perfectly."

11. Keep writing.

12. When your mom offers to teach you how to cook, sew, tile the basement, use power tools, install a ceiling fan, or reverse flush an engine core, do not blow her off.

13. He will be unbelievable. He will exceed every possible expectation of what a young man of seventeen should be able to handle. More people should be like him. But, Al? You have six months. Just that. Six months before your tender romance that is currently full of every pleasure of magical, hopeful youth will turn very, very dark and serious. But he will stay, for years. And he

will hold you and stand by you and you will grow up together. Never stop feeling grateful. Never stop thanking him. Never forget how you loved him or, indeed, how he loved you. And although he is not the One, no one else could have been better right at this moment.

14. Fortune favors the brave. And you are braver than you think.

15. The friends you have right now? They are incredible. In a few months, they will all absolutely blow your mind with loyalty and resilience no seventeen- or eighteen-year-olds should rightly possess.

16. And seriously: buy Frizz Ease.

Pain Pills: A Prologue

It was our first family vacation in years, and it would be our last.

My grandparents Albert and Edna owned a condo in Sarasota, Florida, where, just like the nearly two-thirds of Jewish Detroit, they spent their winters with all the other Midwestern "snowbirds." The condo was modest but glorious—a small two bedroom that smelled of sea salt, right on the Gulf of Mexico with the whitest sand you have ever seen, infinite shells, shuffle board, tennis, and even a swimming pool in the back. Despite scant company for children, Sarasota was warm and breezy and, when Albert and Edna weren't there, it was paradise. We spent a few of our family vacations there in my childhood, but we hadn't returned in years.

We each had our roles when it came to the seaside. My mother was the sun worshipper. Nothing pleased her more than slathering herself in oil and baking in the sun like a true California girl of the 1960s. (Please do not ask me how her skin has never given her a stitch of trouble, nor how she manages to still look thirty years old. It is possible that she drinks the blood of virgins. I am praying I get my fully deserved 50 percent of those genes because the Silber half of the family look like raisins). I was the shade dweller. I had loved the water as a child; you couldn't keep me from diving in with abandon. But, as I grew, so did my water-related anxieties, so I stayed safely on shore, most often in the shade beneath a Joshua tree. My father split the difference. He enjoyed dabbling: a little shore, a little swim, a little stroll, a little Frisbee with anyone he could convince to play with him. But his favorite activity was staring endlessly at the water, contemplating anything and everything. He sometimes did this from his beach chair and sometimes from the terrace of Albert and Edna's condo that overlooked the waves.

The terrace was where I found him that night.

In the haunted early hours of the morning—where it is no longer night but not yet day—I was startled from sleep, suddenly wide awake and anxious. I rose and went out onto the terrace to let the ocean waves calm me until I could sleep again. And there he was.

"Hi Papa," I said, suddenly aware that this moment was sacred. Running into one another in the middle of the night doesn't happen much when you go to boarding school.

He looked up at me and moved a chair closer so that I might sit beside him. I could see a bottle of prescription pills in his hand.

"What's wrong, Dad?" I asked.

"My back feels awful."

"For how long?"

"I don't know, maybe about a month or so?"

I'd never seen him like this. Calm, but not calm.

"I'm . . . " he said, hesitating. "I'm scared to take the pills."

"OK," I said. "Can you tell me why?"

"Because—because pain is supposed to help indicate what is wrong with your body, and if I kill the pain, then I can't figure out what is going on."

He was a problem solver. No big deal: you dive in, you figure out the problem, and then problem solved. But cancer didn't work that way. He'd go in, get the treatments, and then four weeks, four months, four years later, he would still have cancer—and often more cancer, in different places. Cancer would send out its envoys, and cancer colonies would take root. Sometimes cancer would pack up and move out. Sometimes not. This was the first time I had ever seen my father stumped or obviously troubled, and I was so honored that he wasn't hiding it from me. Here in the middle of the night, he was sharing his fear. A full disclosure.

"Well," I said. "What do we know?"

He smiled broadly. "What do we know?" was a Mike Silber catch phrase, his signature tactic to set all the cards out on the table and look at them.

I continued. "OK, we know a few certainties," I said. "First, you are uncomfortable. Discomfort is bad. Second, you want to know what is wrong. That is natural. Assessment: Unless we go to the hospital right now—which we can absolutely do, by the way—I don't think you are going to figure out all of the answers tonight. I am also pretty certain that nothing good comes from a lack of sleep, and you can't sleep if you are in pain. So, all that said, I think you should take the pill now and, in the morning, you will at least be rested enough to make a good decision about the next step."

He looked at me and smiled.

"Yes," he said. "You're right." His expression was a combination of pride and gratitude.

I got up to fetch him a glass of water, beaming. *I am capable*, I thought. *I can make a difference here. I just need to be given an opportunity to help.*

Returning with the water, I asked, "What would Bob say?"

"'I feel good, I feel great, I feel wonderful,'" he said, quoting from our mutual favorite movie, the Bill Murray classic *What About Bob?*

"'I feel good, I feel great, I feel wonderful,'" we said in unison, imitating Bob's opening lines. We laughed and looked at one another.

"Thanks, Al," he said.

It is the only time I ever remember truly contributing to the fight.

The Dying

I brought with me exactly nothing. I had barely gathered my thoughts the day I stopped in the streets of Minneapolis, dropped my books and, zombie-like, got into a taxi to the airport. So when I awoke from the fog, there was nothing to unpack—nothing but the hard realities of every day ahead.

And so I am sleeping in the spare bedroom downstairs tonight, in a pair of light- and dark-blue-checkered pajamas that had been left at the bottom of a reject drawer in my childhood bedroom. Reject pajamas, plus a teal, moth-eaten wool sweater acquired from the dorm share box last spring. Yep. My night-before-the-death outfit is definitely nailing it.

Next to me in bed is Jensen Kent, the Love of My Youth. Kent is asleep next to me, the very fact of which is off, because if Dad were not upstairs dying, he would almost certainly prevent his teenage daughter from lying in bed next to her teenage boyfriend.

But there is nothing funny going on. Kent is asleep, and I am wide-awake and thinking about what must be going on upstairs.

The dying.

I'm also thinking about Bob.

What About Bob? is my undisputed favorite film of all time. In a top-ten list of favorite films, Bob would take up the top three slots. I could watch it on repeat. I could probably quote the entire thing from beginning to end (with intonations and pauses, inflections, music cues, and everything) if you challenged me to. In fact I dare you: challenge me to. Go on.[1]

---

1 I will do it.

First things first:

What About Bob? is a 1991 film directed by Frank Oz about a doctor-patient relationship that goes *way* beyond the office. Bob Wiley (played brilliantly by Bill Murray) is a neurotic psychiatric patient struggling with a whirlwind of paralyzing phobias who, with all the subtlety of crazy-glue, attaches himself to Dr. Leo Marvin (played by the equally astonishing Richard Dreyfuss). He goes to see Dr. Marvin and, in one session, Bob becomes a zealous devotee of Dr. Marvin's latest psychiatric method, detailed in his best-selling book *Baby Steps*. Bob bonds with and comes to depend upon Dr. Marvin so much that—in the most charming way conceivable—Bob follows his doctor on his month-long vacation in New Hampshire.

Dr. Marvin wants a few weeks of rest and relaxation because he is preparing for a big interview on *Good Morning America*—a needy patient who can't take a hint is the last thing he needs! Thus Dr. Marvin demands that Bob return home to New York. But Bob decides to stay to indulge in his very own "vacation from his problems," and remains in the area. While Dr. Marvin is driven increasingly insane, Marvin's neighbors, wife, daughter, and death-obsessed son Sigmund all take to Bob's openness, loopy charm, self-effacing humor, and sense of fun—none of which Dr. Marvin himself possesses.

Let's first get a few things clear:

→ I did *not* play it so many times on VHS that it began to skip.

→ I have *never* claimed that *Bob* is the *I Ching*. Not ever.

→ I have *not* quoted *Bob* to total strangers on public transportation.

→ I do *not* love it so much that sometimes I put it on just as wallpaper while I clean the house or do my taxes.

→ I did *not* get so frustrated by my inability to access Bob's amusement and wisdom at all times that I resorted to holding a professional (purpose-bought) microphone up to

the television speaker to record the entire film on a 120-
minute audio cassette so that I might listen to it on my
Walkman . . . or in the car . . . or at summer camp . . .

Any of those things might mean that I was an obsessive, crazy fool. So
. . . yes . . . OK. The truth is that I am a fool for *What About Bob?* and I
don't care who knows it.

When listing favorite films, I have always considered it important to
designate and divide into separate categories: The Favorite Films That
Are Legitimate Works of Art and Really Challenge You List— *Citizen
Kane* and *Schindler's List*-y films that are inarguably brilliant but require
focus and discipline and serious-mindedness. And the Special Favorite
Films You Could Watch Again and Again Because They Make You Feel
Amazing List—which includes things like *The Great Muppet Caper* and
The Jerk. Sometimes there is a crossover (*Amelie*). But the point is that
I think everybody has a film or two like *Bob*: the kind of favorite movie
you love so much that the second it ends, you could press rewind and
watch the whole damn thing again.

I know people who irrationally love *Big*. I know people who can quote
the entirety of *National Lampoon's European Adventure*. I know a handful of people who can't get enough of *Turner and Hooch*.[2] Well, for our
family, it was *What About Bob?* and it all started with Dad. I was nine
years old the first time we ever watched it in the last home we ever had
in Los Angeles, on Bedford Drive in Beverly Hills. He practically sprinted
out to purchase the VHS the day it came out, and we watched it twice,
back to back.

Dad loved this movie for reasons I may never fully know and desperately wish I did. Perhaps it had something to do with the odd take on psy-
chiatry. Perhaps it had to do with Bob's innocence, or Bill Murray's irreverent but childlike sense of humor that reminded me so much of Dad's.
Perhaps it was because the film has a really touching central message, but
doesn't take itself too seriously. Perhaps it was just amusing; I truly don't

---

2   I've learned never to underestimate the devotion inspired by Tom Hanks.

know, but the film became important to me because it was important to him. We would watch it together, laugh, quote, laugh some more, and as I grew, *Bob* took on its very own significance.

When I woke up in the morning Dad would often greet me with: "Good morning, Gil . . . I said *good morning, Gil.*"

Or the casual greeting of "Ahoy!"

If someone asked how he felt about something, he might respond with: "There are two types of people in this world: those who like Neil Diamond and those who don't."

When someone was mean to me at school, he would quote Bob's wisdom: "You know, I treat people as if they were telephones. If I meet somebody I think doesn't like me I say to myself, I say, 'Bob, this one is temporarily out of order.' You know, don't break the connection, just hang up and try again!"

Therein lies the allure of *What About Bob?* Bob Wiley, it would seem, is oddly enlightened, and *What About Bob?* is oddly profound. With each re-viewing of this 90s comedy, I discovered another level of meaning, a deeper sense of universal profundity. This comic insanity mixed with penetrating insight is a quality only such genius clowns like Bill Murray seem to be capable of portraying: those rare comedians so in touch with life's harsh truths, that they make it their mission to (brilliantly) cultivate laughter. And every time I watch *Bob*, I not only felt smarter or wiser, but I felt closer to my dad.

About two-thirds of the way into the film, we find Bob sleeping over at the Marvins' Lake Winnipesaukee home due to a torrential rainstorm. He shares a room with Siggy, Dr. Marvin's eleven-year-old son. They lie there in their PJs, in angled twin beds, staring into the darkness. Siggy looks terrified:

SIGGY: Bob?
BOB: Yeah?
SIGGY: Are you afraid of death?

Bob is caught off guard. He is suddenly frightened, too—his eyes grow wide and searching, like a child trying to keep his cool.

BOB: Yeah.

(It's a "yeah" as in a "Yeah, so?"—a way particular to children one-upping each other.)

   SIGGY: Me, too. And there's no way out of it. You're going to die. I'm
      going to die. It's going to happen.

(Siggy blinks; clearly the fear is very, very real.)

   SIGGY: And who cares if it's tomorrow or eighty years? Much sooner
      in your case. Do you know how fast time goes? I was six, like,
      yesterday.
   BOB: Me, too.
   SIGGY: I'm going to die. You are going to die. What else is there to be
      afraid of?

And so I think. I think about The Dying.

In that moment, as I lie downstairs in ratty checkered pajamas beside Kent, that very scene from that very stupid, over-quoted, over-played, trivial and pathetically beloved movie is all I can think of.

My dad is going to die.

There is no way out of it.

And who cares if it really is tomorrow or in eighty years?

It is going to happen.

And if he dies, I am very certain that I might die, too.

Siggy is right; What else is there to be afraid of?

Al(ex(andra)) and Lilly

I was ten years old the first time I went away to summer camp, and I remember many things about that summer. I remember the simultaneous terror and thrill of being truly on my own for the first time. I remember my Winnie-the-Pooh bedsheets, music everywhere, the glory of the lakes, the mysterious smells from Pinecrest cafeteria, and new friends from foreign places.

I remember waking up one morning and realizing that I hadn't thought about cancer in two weeks.

But above all, I remember that on the first day my counselor asked all of us for our nicknames. I paused when it was my turn.

Now, I love the name Alexandra. It's a name with grandeur, with presence. But long names on little people seem to make people a little uneasy, because for the first ten years of my life, people kept calling me "Alex." Don't get me wrong—I'm not Alex-ist. Some of my best friends are called Alex. It's just not me.

This was my chance to pick the right name, wipe "Alex" clear off the face of the map, and become myself. And for me, the right name was "Al." Maybe Al sounds more like a middle-aged plumber than a big-haired ten-year-old at her first theater camp. But what can I say; it felt right.

"Hello, my name is Alexandra . . . but you can call me Al," I said hesitantly, trying it out, my heart throbbing.

Everyone smiled, and the counselor took down the name tag she had made for my closet and flipped it over, writing *A-L* in big block letters before refastening it to the door.

I never looked back. I was Al for the whole of that summer, and it was magical. And when I came back the following summer—after a whole year of being "actually my name is . . . no, Alex is fine," back home in Detroit—I walked into my cabin and there "AL" was, already on my closet.

And then of course, there was Lilly.

I can't say that I remember the first time I ever met Lilly (Isn't that how most friendships start?), but what I *can* say is that there never seemed to be a time at Interlochen when she wasn't somewhere in the landscape. We both first attended Interlochen the summer we both turned eleven and, somewhere along the line, we crossed paths in a modern dance class. We were both badass little eleven-year-olds, prancing across the dance building on the banks of Green Lake, feeling our Martha Graham feelings in identical black unitards. Back then, I had no idea what Lilly would come to mean to me.

Lilly's full name is Lillian Townsend Copeland. (And no, she was not related to Aaron Copland, though she still enjoys referring to him as "Old Uncle Aaron."[3])

We had both decided to upgrade from summer camp to yearlong enrollment at Interlochen Arts Academy in Michigan. We were both overachievers—her in oboe, me in theater—and we shared a dorm suite in our senior year with two other theater majors, Cristina and Courtney. The four of us became the Four Amigos (T-shirts were made), but it was our reign as Possibly Interlochen's Worst Ever Hall Assistants that bonded me and Lilly together for life.

I'm not saying we were abysmal. I am merely saying that one could take a convicted arsonist, give him a pack of matches, escort him to the log cabin of his childhood nemesis, instruct him to "have a good time," and the predictably charred evening would be preferable to having Lilly and me be responsible for you in high school.

We were likely hall assistant candidates, I suppose: returning "lifers"

---

3   Lilly's version of Copeland has an E, Aaron, no E.

who "bled blue"— terms used for students who had been at Interlochen as long as anyone could remember, and thus bled the uniform colors: light blue on top (with a visible collar), navy blue on the bottom (students became more and more creative with these uniform rules as the school year progressed).

Our dormitory, known as Thor Johnson House or "TJ" for short, was charming it its way—a common area, two levels of dorm rooms above a basement designated for laundry and practice rooms. The walls were plastered with handmade posters for *Sleeping Beauty*, visual art showings, poetry readings, movie nights and, idiosyncratic Michigan-isms such as reminders to "Wear bright colors during hunting season!" TJ was connected to the campus cafeteria, thus constantly smelled of "cooking in bulk," as well as of microwave popcorn, toast, laundry, hormones, and teenaged artistic ambition.

As HAs, Lilly and I were supposed to make certain everyone was comfortable, felt at home, and had a place to talk if they needed to. That was the part we were good at—the social, caring big sister stuff! We could help plan a medium-sized hall party; we could make sure the Chinese piano major who doesn't speak English gets everything she needs in order to find her way to class on Monday.[4] We could help the girl who just moved from South Africa and was apart from her childhood boyfriend for the first time. That stuff.

But we also had to attend HA meetings about house life, vote on house policies, make certain everyone in our hall attended the big school community meetings held every Thursday before lunch.

We had to clean things and organize community service.

We had to make sure everyone was present in a fire drill.

We had to attend the fire drill.

We had to have not pulled the fire alarm ourselves.

We had to be good examples. We had to be quiet. We had to obey the rules. We had to not have an illegal television (with a VHS player!) hiding in a giant Tupperware.

---

4   Have I mentioned that the classrooms at Interlochen were in an actual forest?

We had to not get involved in the Great Paint Plot. But come on, who wouldn't get involved with a Great Paint Plot?

Our roommate Cristina and her friend Ellie from down the hall, in a flurry of senioritis, had decided to paint their naked torsos with red and turquoise tempera paint, walk around the entire dorm (during school hours, so even teachers and boys might see them), and videotape it.

And who tagged along? Our entire dorm. And who videotaped it? Your friendly local HAs, Al and Lilly. And how does this videotape end? With our (incredibly cool, but also incredibly adult) dorm leader Angela, staring deadpan into the camera and simply saying, "No." Then she looks at Cristina, Ellie, and our entire entourage and repeats, "*No*—no no no." Then it cuts out.

Oops.

Five minutes after we were caught, we were back in our room, with the sun setting over Green Lake outside our window. Cristina and Ellie were wearing T-shirts and looks of mild shame; Courtney was crumpled in our womb chair in the corner, and Lilly and I were standing, military style, in front of Angela as she explained that she knew we had six weeks of senior year left but we all really need to get a grip on ourselves. "I love all of you so much but seriously. COME. ON."

We all nodded.

She continued. "Additionally, Alexandra Michelle and Lillian Townsend, you are hall assistants! You are supposed to be *leaders*, set *examples*; you are supposed to be the first line of defense when all the parents paying thousands of dollars and visiting from Asia want to know where on earth they have sent their children."

She was right.

Angela continued, "I can't believe I am about to say this—I literally cannot believe I am about to say the following sentence—but please, *please* do not cover your naked bodies in paint, roam the public hallways during working (or nonworking) hours, and please, please do not videotape it."

We nodded again.

"Angela?" Cristina said, lifting her head. "There is just something I want to get off my chest."

"Please say it is not your shirt."

"Yes! I mean no! I just—" Cristina said. "We're sorry."

We really were.

Some people might have been intimidated to share their dorm life with three boisterous theater majors, but not Lilly. Lilly was an honorary theater major: she had drama and flair, she was theatrical and powerful, and she loved it. Sure, sometimes she didn't want to talk about Tennessee Williams anymore. Sure, she may have gotten irritated at Cristina and me doing vocal warm ups in our communal shower for the millionth time. Sure, she may have been on the brink of killing us all if she heard us talk about theater department politics one more time. And maybe sometimes she despaired of having to explain music major basics to us, like the time she had to explain to Courtney that the "beeping box" that so fascinated her was in fact a metronome.

But if she ever truly contemplated roommate-icide, she never showed it. "Do your theater stuff," she would say and just keep on making her reeds and doing her homework. More often than not, she'd join right in, picking out our outfits for auditions, expressing her monologue preferences, and, most memorably of all, helping me learn every single line and lyric as I prepared to play Amalia Balash in *She Loves Me*.

"I think you need to be a little sobbier," she'd said.

"Lilly, if I got any 'sobbier,' I'd be Meg Ryan."

"Well, then sob away—you'd have a cute haircut and quite a career."

How we loved Lilly. How could we not? We loved her bewitching voice with the Southern drawl that only came out when she was exhausted. We loved the way she hated making reeds but dutifully made them anyway. We loved the short hair she sometimes wore in little pigtails that looked something like the sprigs on top of Pebbles's head. When we asked her why she wore it that way, she replied, "Um . . . because I look cute."

In the first week of school, all auditions for the coming semester take place—theater majors audition for the first two shows of the season, voice majors get placed in their studios, dance majors are cast in the winter ballet, and the instrumentals audition the entire week for their chair in the orchestra.

I suppose this is the point where I let you in on a little secret: Lilly is so insanely talented at the oboe, so gifted a musical artist, that some might call it unjust. To listen to Lilly play is like listening to a person sing— actually sing through their instrument, with all of the individuality and soulfulness of a raw, vital, pulsing human voice that manages to capture the beauty of existence just as film captures an image, or honey captures light.

The only person who does not understand Lilly's genius is Lilly. The day the chairs were posted, Lilly lay in, buried in her duvet, distraught that she had blown it—thus ruining her senior year, her chances at getting into college, and possibly her entire life.

The rest of the suite woke up early to look at the posting for her— certain of her impending success. We screamed and celebrated in the main lobby, jumping up and down in characteristically un-music-major-like fashion. We flew upstairs, burst in, and jumped on Lilly screaming like the lunatics we were. "First chair, Lilly! First fucking chair!"

Lilly sat up and rubbed her eyes, then beamed.

So the Four Amigos had a lot of adventures that year at Interlochen, and together we all went to MORP[5] on a great big yellow school bus: Cristina and I in vintage gowns, Lilly in an original dress my mom had designed, and the ever avant-garde Courtney in her own gown made of duct tape.

But Lilly was something else.

Virtuosic musical gift aside, Lilly is rife with what I like to call "goods." I will now list them (because I love both Lilly and lists). It doesn't take a genius to notice that Lillian Copeland has the biggest, most gorgeous hazel eyes you've ever seen. But let me tell you something else: this girl is compassionate, capable, and feisty. She looks right at you and waves sneakily with her oboe during the orchestral bow when you are standing

---

5   The Interlochen version of Prom. MORP is "Prom" backwards.

and screaming for her solo. She doesn't refer to her oboe as "the oboe," but rather as "Oboe," as if "Oboe" is his/her[6] name. She is the just right amount of perfectionist and sees the great virtue in "being cute." And yes, OK, fine: she has killer legs with perfect ankles that look amazing in heels.

But, reader? Lilly is the kind of solid you only think is possible in *pioneer women*. With a sense of empathy so intuitive it makes you ache.

She was my very closest friend. She was the only one I truly spoke with about my dad's increasingly concerning illness when the going got tough. And it did get tough.

Dad started out the year with his fifth round of regular chemo in the span of nine years. (If there is such a thing as "regular.") He was in good shape overall. A bald head was the only giveaway of his illness. Otherwise, Dad was an ox—six foot three inches of pure, Herculean, I-have-cancer-but-remain-symptom-free-for-a-decade type of strength. No one saw the end coming. No one.

That somehow made it all the more ruthless.

---

6   I am not certain if Oboe has a gender.

Kent

The Night Before, I lie awake beside a sleeping Kent.
Kent, who always smelled vaguely of the ocean.
Kent, with his kiss deep and knowing.
Kent, whose sacrifice still reverberates in my marrow.

I hadn't always loved Jensen Kent.

In the beginning, we were just friends. First, because he was friendly, and second, because I was already dating a boy named Jeremey who was in every way my "motorcycle guy" and first rebellion.

For you see, I never rebelled. I was a squeaky clean kid, terrified that any trespass into the gnarly world of adolescence might only add further to the already crushing daily burdens endured by my parents. This took such things as "growing up" and "having needs" off the table of possible options. This was how such things as being publically shamed by my middle school art teacher, high school bullying, and, my favorite, hiding my menstrual period *for a year*, went largely un-discussed.

Not that either one of my parents were in any way *actually* scary. I was merely scared of my own volition; a perfectionist almost crippled by the terror of error, for to disappoint—or, more crucially, to *burden* them further—would have been a weight too great to bear. I rigorously took on the task of providing my parents with a perfect child: a singular source of hope and joy and promise. It was in this internal atmosphere that I smothered myself, believing in my bones that any problem, mistake, even the tiniest of transgressions, was my contribution to *not* curing cancer.

Driven by this crippling need I got straight As, excelled in my extracurricular activities, had a few virtuous friends, avoided growing up and all its curiosities, and frenetically overachieved. As the self-appointed hope, future, pleasure, reason, and shared source of my parents' reason to keep fighting, I took it upon myself to provide my parents with every excessive joy and pride imaginable. There was no one else to share the task with, and I was operating in a vacuum of frantic desperation. I learned that no one asks if you are in pain or in trouble if you have a resume full of achievements. I was panic-stricken that the entire world would collapse if I did not succeed.

When I did socialize, it was one-on-one or in intensely G-rated settings. Safe. Hermetically sealed. I needed to be in control of everything I could to avoid making mistakes. Because of that, I spent a great deal of time alone. I filled that empty space with achievement, creativity, books, ideas, and huge imaginative worlds that required no playmate.

My parents wanted me to have as normal a childhood as possible. They kept me away from the bulk of my father's health issues. Who could blame them? So, achieve I did. In my young mind, *achievement* was the only contribution I could offer to making Dad well again.

I returned to Interlochen for my Senior year in the fall of 2000, with big hopes and plans for the future, not to mention a boyfriend acquired the previous school year. I also had a revelation: that my pierced, leather-jacket-wearing, punk-music-listening, left-handed, red-headed, pseudo-intellectual boyfriend was my small way of rebelling.

As mentioned before, junior-year-boyfriend Jeremey was my "motorcycle guy." He was an assertion of my independence now that I was away from home full time, free to explore with my own judgments and moral compass. After an initial flurry of phone calls between my parents and Interlochen begging *any* adult to step in and end the relationship, my parents resigned themselves to the fact that the universe was not going to implode if I loved a rebellious redhead with one too many Es in his name.

It turned out that my parents needn't have worried, as it couldn't last with the bad boy forever. Jeremey graduated and got out into the big bad world and in truth, I don't think he fully understood what was happening to my father and my family, nor did I have any ability to fully share it. Eventually, in a spectacularly ordinary teenage manner, we just parted ways.

I suppose that was where Kent entered in.

He was a friend first, and a true one. When I arrived for my senior year at Interlochen, I was a returning student but Kent was at the Academy for his very first time, to attend the final year of high school. It was a common practice. Opening weekend, his WASP-y, dry, New Englander mother and father (both doctors—of nuclear physics and astrophysics, respectively) escorted him, wandering the campus with horror-struck curiosity. This arts school perfectly defined exactly the kind of free-spirited, tree-swinging, paint-covered human they did not want their son to be. *This is not the yacht club*, their American Gothic facial expressions said, *and this black sheep in our family is going to an Ivy League School if it kills us all.*

But Kent fit in perfectly. Interlochen had its own hierarchies both theater-department- and campus-wide, and Kent managed to carve himself a comfortable little throne in both. He deftly won over the theater department because he was talented, incredibly, bright and, crucially, *tall*. He got fantastic roles right off the bat and was a "good catch" as far as scene partners were concerned. On campus he was charismatic, confident, wickedly funny, and handsome (he wore his hair in a long, gorgeous ponytail he cut during winter break) and I observed his blossoming popularity from afar, with the cool distance of "having a boyfriend."

But as the year thundered along, changes came—at home, at school, with Jeremey, with my father's health. And somehow, as the year progressed, my friendship with Kent became the kind of friendship people write novels about.

He called me to catch up over Christmas break. I remember Dad taking the first call and, looking at the caller ID (before caller ID automatically listed the location), saying "631? What is 631?" (Dad had *Rain Man*-like knowledge of little things like this.) "631 is Long Island! *Long Island?* That must be the ponytailed guy! I like him!" I was surprised that my stomach flipped at the prospect of talking with my friend (and nothing more) over the phone. But it did. I filed it away under "Teenager," sub-category "Shared Experiences," sub-subcategory "Boarding School," and left that file there to gather dust.

But after we returned from the holidays, my heart sank when I learned Kent had started dating someone else. I cared for them both, was genuinely happy for them, and didn't want to interfere. Plus, despite feeling further and further away from my boyfriend in college, I was still devoted to him.

Furthermore, Dad was not well. His health was failing. There were no overt signs, but something was in the air. I was a busy, driven, ambitious high school senior who had no time for distractions.

Yet, by spring break, Kent and I had not only been paired in our Shakespeare scenes as Antony and Cleopatra, but also cast opposite one another in *As You Like It*. It would be a springtime full of Shakespeare, poetry, and honest conversations, all with Kent. Love crept up on us.

Kent and I had the spring. A fleeting, perfect spring of youthful flushes, stolen kisses, and dreams. Spring turned to summer, summer to fall: a perfect six months of young love.

There was so much shared before Dad collapsed at graduation. Before his new treatment that rendered him unable to walk, or breathe, or stay awake. Before we both had to grow up very, very quickly.

It was everything that you hope and dream of, and should ever be so lucky to have when you are seventeen and truly in love for the first time and it is spring.

The Morning

I'd been trying to go to college in Minneapolis. I was trying to trust the faculty and my by then ex-boyfriend Jeremey, who was (awkwardly) in the class ahead of me, that this could set me up for a meaningful life that wouldn't disappoint anyone. I was trying to find my footing. I was trying not to miss Kent too much. I was trying to not worry too much about what was going on at home.

I tried. I did. But I wasn't doing any of it very well.

As mentioned before, my parents shielded me from the bulk of the cancer difficulties. But as time wore on I felt more than merely protected from it; I felt shut out. What was appropriate to shield from a nine-year-old didn't feel appropriate to keep from a teenager, and I don't think any of us understood how to transition in this area of our family. Before we all knew it, I was "old enough." But I didn't know what to ask or how to help and, at least I think, they simultaneously didn't want to burden me and didn't want me to bear witness to its indignities. I felt as though I were outside a locked door—ear pressed against the heavy wood, able to hear only the murmurs from within. Somehow, all three of us had lost the key.

Operating in this vacuum, it is an understatement to say that I was not doing well at college. I loved my small class of thirteen actors, the faculty, the classes. I loved the university environment and was still managing to pull good grades, much to my astonishment. But I longed for Kent and all of my Interlochen friends. Most of all, I was coming apart with doubts about home and the elephant that no one was talking about: my father was dying.

I worked at Interlochen the summer following graduation—Kent and Lilly were there too, along with many of our friends, and it felt like a meaningful transition to a permanent goodbye. Furthermore, Mom and Dad had decided it was time to try an experimental treatment at MD Anderson—a hospital specializing in oncology treatments in Houston, Texas. Dad was going to participate in a trial for a very new but very intense chemotherapy, the kind used on Lance Armstrong to great success. This didn't faze me—Dad had been knocking back chemo like Jell-O shots for years. I offered to stay home and help, but my father was both sentimental as well as prideful and didn't want to "rob me" of the summer before college; nor, do I think, did he want me to bear witness to his struggles.

At the end of that summer, I had returned home to a disintegrated father. I had just days leading up to my departure for college. We went to eat at a deli on Thirteen Mile. It was tense. Dad was in bad shape. He was weak and frail. I was so underinformed about what was going on—and thus so angry, confused, and frustrated with cancer—that I ended up taking it out on the vessel holding the disease. Dad mentioned that he was afraid to sleep. I snapped, "Why are you afraid to fall asleep?" and he yelled back, "Because I'm afraid I am going to die!" The deli went quiet. People turned. I stood up and walked out and circled the building three times. No tears. Just primal, absolute fear.

Then Dad's birthday on the first of September.

Meanwhile, I was writing longhand letters to Kent, who was taking a year off to work on a dairy farm, his hours so different from mine that we never truly got a chance to speak on the rotary phone Kent shared with two Portuguese farm workers, Clibbs and Roderigo.[7]

Then September 11.

---

7   No, but seriously.

Meanwhile, my ex-boyfriend Jeremey was after me for explanations and retribution and forgiveness. He was insistent and merciless. It was always all about him. He was everywhere I was in Minneapolis and it was quickly wearing me out.

Then my parents' anniversary.

At school, I was studying sociology and Shakespeare and philosophy as well as writing papers and participating in lectures. I was living alone in a single coffin-like room in the corner of the thirteenth floor in a massive dormitory. I ran up and down the flights of stairs to combat my anxiety. I called home, but no one was there to answer and when they were, Mom was a ghost of herself. I could hear it in her voice; the tense act of hope her positive words and tight voice were performing, and I wished she would just tell me—and admit to herself—the truth.

I lasted about eight weeks in Minneapolis. It wasn't meant to be. On Monday, October 8th, 2001, I was walking to class and I stopped dead: I knew that I had to go home that day.

So I did.

There I was, back in Michigan, temporarily relieved, but now a visitor in the strange house of a dying person—pills, machines, the smell of hospital, and dread. Unfamiliar people were there offering opinions and advice no one wanted as they wiped their brows, relieved it wasn't their time to go. My mother, having arranged for Kent to fly in, was preoccupied running up and down the stairs being hostess, hospice nurse, and everything in between. And the most unbelievable feeling came over me. I was furious.

There were so many things I thought I would have felt—distress, fear, despair. But I was engulfed by rage. How could I have no idea things had gotten so bad? And so quickly? Was I so much of a child still that I was not granted the dignity of this information? Was I a member of this family? Or was I simply the child of a couple fighting cancer?

I felt lanced straight through the gut with total isolation; there was no one to call. My parents were the people who were both horrifically afflicted and who had all the information. I felt patronized. I felt terrified.

I felt angry. When you do not have the information, you cannot be granted a choice. My father might have wanted to face the harsh realities in solitude with my mother, to keep the terror from me, to allow me to remain on my path. I see the logic now, but then I raged that I hadn't been given time to prepare. I might have made more memories, said more loving things, come home more. But I had been robbed of the chance.

I seethed.

No wonder Kent is coming, I thought. *He is here to look after me because Mom is looking after Dad, and this is all suddenly very clear. I am a terrible person in the middle of a situation I do not understand and, now that I do, I cannot tolerate it.*

When Kent arrived, I went numbly upstairs with him. Dad was laying down in bed, grasping for every breath he could as the cancer was winning inside his ravaged body. He smiled weakly as Kent and I entered.

"Hi, Kent. How's the farm?"

Kent sat down in a bedside chair and Dad took his hand.

"Good," Kent smiled, chuckling a little. This chuckle was Kent's signature, rolling and tentative and sad.

"Good," Dad said and closed his eyes, spent.

Then it was my turn.

There was nothing to say. I don't believe we said a word. But he gripped my hand with Herculean strength, as if the only part of his entire being still able to communicate the power of his desires were his strong, gigantic hands—clutching at those he loved, at the words he was desperate to say and possibly anchoring him to life itself. He reached across his body and gripped tighter with his other hand, until both sets of our hands were knotted together and pulsing. I think he was embarrassed. I think he was sorry. I think he wanted me to know how much he loved me, and I think he wanted me to go.

I dropped my head, placing my forehead on the mountain of our hands and lingered there for a moment before standing up and walking away.

I suppose that was my goodbye—insufficient, wordless, collapsed—but, if that was what it would continue to be, I didn't want to build up a collection of memories of Michael Silber in that state. I would prefer to preserve the memories I already had and not tarnish them with how it was at the end.

Kent and I headed downstairs. There were strangers waiting in our living room, all of them saying unthinkable things: *This is the end of course. Oh isn't it awful being in a house where you can feel death looming? It reminds me of being in a hospital only you don't feel nearly as clean. Oh, shh shh the daughter is coming! Don't say anything, just be pleasant.*

I stared at them at the base of the stairs and left through the front door without a word. Kent and I headed to a deli, ate, and returned home in silence to a silent house. Mom was spent, and suggested I stay downstairs beside Kent. In hindsight, I suppose it was partly for my comfort, for me to be held at night, but also partly to keep me from the horrors inside the bedroom.

I woke in the middle of the night with stabbing pains in my chest. I couldn't breathe. I needed air. I needed help. My chest constricting, I left the bed and made my way upstairs to my parents' room and found the door closed.

It was then that I remembered. I remembered about The Dying. I needed to pull myself together on my own. I entered my childhood bathroom next door, and folded over, I counted my breaths—*in 2, 3, 4, out, 2, 3, 4*—but the pain kept stabbing, crushing my breast, turning my heart to pulp. *What is happening?* I thought.

I attempted to stand and failed. I crawled to the door of my parents' room, struggled to my feet and placed my hand upon the door, preparing to knock.

But then, I heard it: the cries of the final hours.

Cathy, my father gasped in desperation, *I love you . . . I love you . . .*

There were rustles and machines and steps and broken voices.

. . . I love you . . .

With that, the pains in my chest ceased instantly. I slid slowly down the wall beside the door, my hand still placed upon it and, as I sat there, listening to the final moments, I wept to be missing it, knowing it was a door, an inch, a knock, a *breath* away, but not for me to witness. I found myself in real time, in those final moments, inside the middle of a long-felt metaphor:

I was listening to my parents' love story reach its conclusion, just as I was meant to, outside a door.

Drenched in a pool of sweat, my face almost imperceptibly contorting with the knowledge of the night, I realized the pain was no accident. No pain is.

. . . *I love you* . . .

( )

Later that morning, I awoke again, back in my bed. There was rustling in the house—feet shuffling and hushed voices. I felt over to my right for Kent, but he was not there, though his space was still warm and imprint fresh. The door to the bedroom was shut.

I shot out of bed and moved to the closed door—wanting to burst through, to smash it open and run but I stopped. Hesitating, I put my hand upon the knob, knowing that on the other side of the door lay the rest of my life. As long as I remained in the bedroom downstairs, I could keep reality at bay, even if only for a moment or two. But I held my breath and turned the knob, placing my ear to a crack I had made in the doorway. Kent was on the phone upstairs in the kitchen.

"He's dead," I heard him say.

I was seared—forever scored by these words that went into me like a branding iron, unforgettable and irreversible. There was the separation of life before and life after those words. What would I preserve of those last 6,673 days? *Eighteen years, three months, six days, give or take a few hours.* Would I remember every second of what is now my personal BCE—everything that was "before he died?" *953 weeks and two days* . . . What was I meant to keep?

And then I was overcome with a relief I would continue to feel guilty about for years. The suffering and struggle and indignities of The Dying had finally ended. For him. For all of us. I was relieved, and for that I am sorry.

I don't remember what I did next. I don't remember the next moment I looked into Kent's face. Or my mother's.

There are some things that happened that morning before I woke that I will never know, and I frankly do not want to. Things Kent and my mother shared in those final moments that I am certain they will take to their own graves. Things that are dark and hard and eternal.

I walked calmly upstairs to my bedroom. In the next room, my father lay dead behind his still-closed bedroom door. I opened my closet, took off my checkered pajamas and teal wool sweater and folded them in a neat pile, and then I pulled on a long dress of pure white silk.

I wanted to be ready to act. I wanted to always remember what I wore that day. And I wanted it to be beautiful. Hopeful.

I remember wanting to be armed in white.

Planning

I recall, probably more vividly than any other, the moment Lilly heard that Dad was gone. Kent and I were seated on my bed, both stoic. I wanted to be there when he told her, but I did not want to do it myself.

I don't remember what he said, but I do remember the depth of the wail I could hear through the telephone, and how much I envied it.

She loved him. Everyone did.

They can only be described as the Funeral People, and they were retrieving Dad's corpse and carrying it down the stairs with what I considered to be an overstated sense of stoicism.

"Hey!" I wanted to shout "Hey you! All of you tall serious men in black suits and frowning faces. *Hey*! Are you listening to me? You are very odd men, all of you, which I suppose you have to be. After all, I've never quite understood how or why anyone really gets into, you know, the Business. Now while I am certain you are extremely capable and you run The Dying like a real tight ship, please! This is not that serious! Laugh, smile, be of good cheer!"

But the men obviously weren't listening to my inner monologue; they were too busy carting my father's body downstairs.

The Funeral People moved down the stairs and through the front door. The doors to the hearse opened, then closed. The Main Funeral Guy shook our hands, handed us a card, closed the door behind him, and told us to show up somewhere later that day. It was like a Dentist Appointment of Death, just without the free oral hygiene swag.

The second they left, the house was filled with an immediate flurry of activity. We fussed ourselves with practicalities. Kent and I only let my mother make the phone calls that were necessary for her to make—family ones, sentimental ones, the ones where she could come apart in safety. The remaining 8,000 phone calls we did ourselves.

Kent got my mom's address book and asked whom "her people" were. Nancy—her college roommate. Amanda—her good friend in San Francisco. Uncle Mikey—her baby brother who lived in Kansas City. Fran and Ken—our best family friends who lived in the area. Assorted other local friends and neighbors.

In the meantime, I went about calling a list of friends who were now spread all across the country, creating a kind of phone tree. The awkward conversations that followed went like this: "Hi there. It's Al . . . I'm—not great. Sorry to kamikaze you with this but um . . . so my dad actually died . . . I—I know. Yeah, I'm pretty numb and in high-functioning mode. Yeah, don't panic. I am sure that I will start feeling it at some point. But look, can you come to Detroit? The funeral is on Friday. Great . . . And can you call Haley and Neil and Aaron and tell them too? Because I don't really want to. Thank you . . . I love you, too."

So the good thing was that *my* people were on the way. Lilly would be there later that night. Cristina and Courtney took the Greyhound from Pittsburgh. Jeremey was on his way from Minneapolis. Grey, one of my best friends from Interlochen, was to arrive late that afternoon. One friend was flying from Boston. Another—who had long ago promised he would be there when this inevitable day came—was coming in from Brown. Friends came in from Chicago and Salt Lake.

And there was a whole busload of people still at Interlochen who were driving down just for the occasion. Michael Arden, fatherless himself, agreed to sing in the ceremony and cried on the phone (a rare occurrence), telling me "I felt like he was my dad," followed immediately by, "Also, I love you so much, I'm flying *Spirit*."

As the information came in, Kent and I began compiling an exponentially growing list of all of the arrivals and of the people that would be fetching and delivering and housing those people. Before long there was a chart.

"The funeral home called," said Kent. "Apparently we need to show up and 'deal with things.'"

"How long do we have?" I asked looking at my mother and Kent.

"We should take care of everything as soon as possible."

Which meant we needed to be there by noon.

Kent continued. "Also, your grandparents called. They said your dad's service needs to be done in a synagogue."

Okay, so I guess we should add "find a rabbi and a synagogue" to the To-Do list.

If lions have their prides and fish have their schools, there was a screech of Silbers sitting in that dull, gray room at the funeral home later that day. This funeral home, though professional and all, did not so much succeed in showing respect for the dead as it failed to make you want to live. Or perhaps it was the company.

First were my grandfather Albert—a lawyer and a silent, loveless patriarch, possibly an undiagnosed narcissist—and my grandmother Edna—a depressive, pint-sized former piano teacher and incredible sculptor who had once been a beauty and was possibly a pathological liar. The day before, my father had begged to see his parents at his deathbed. Both had refused. That morning, as his corpse lay in the bed, Edna managed to stand outside the doorway and look in for a few seconds before darting back down to the living room. Albert remained in the living room, refusing to even go upstairs. Then there was Uncle Eli, the second born, my handsome but slightly psychedelic-drug-addled uncle, an extremely gifted musician who played any and all forms of guitar. There was Aunt Deborah, the undisputed doyenne of American and Amish quilting, along with her extremely antagonistic life partner, Joyce. I had always liked Deborah—she had advocated for my theatrical interests, and she had even dragged her parents to come see me in plays.[8] Deborah also went through a decade or so of deep hatred for her parents in early adulthood and was, in my memory, a fairly angry person.

None of the Silbers were very pleasant to begin with. They were made less pleasant still when they learned that my father's final wishes were for his body to be cremated. *Ruh-roh*.

In Judaism, cremation is forbidden. By Jewish Law, Jews are required to bury a body as soon as possible after and as close as possible to the location of death. The respect and honor that must be accorded the body of a *niftar* (someone who has passed away) is in some ways greater than the respect we might accord that person when he was alive.

For Jews, the human body is the physical element in a complex and ultimately spiritual being. The human body is not simply the housing for the spirit, it is part and parcel of the combined human being—a being that will ultimately exist in greater spiritual form in the World to Come, when the Messiah comes. The body, insofar as Judaism sees it, is more than a casing or a vessel for the soul; it exceeds the function of a husk and therefore demands our gratitude and utmost respect.

And in that vein, a remaining living person must see to it that a *niftar* is buried with that respect. It is considered to be the ultimate good deed (or *mitzvah*), for doing a good deed for the dead is a greater deed than doing one for the living, because there is always the chance that the living person might one day repay you. A dead person cannot return favors. They are dead; therefore, anything you do for them is pure altruism.

All of that is great and good and moral and righteous and many, many other things I respect deeply about Jews and Judaism and human nature

---

8   Also, in recent years, I hear she has seen me a few times on Broadway, but came and went without telling me.

in general. But as far as I understood it on October 9, 2001, no one in this room was an actual, practicing, religious Jew. *No one.*

Albert and Edna Silber were secular Jews. Jew-*ish*, if you will—culturally Jewish, certainly, and as far as I knew at the time, they did not appear to observe or practice the faith-based aspects of Judaism regularly, or have a relationship with God. I don't recall a single Shabbat, Hanukkah gathering, or Passover Seder, and I definitely don't recall a Yom Kippur breaking of the fast. The Silbers took enormous issue with my mother's non-Jewish status, not because I believe it actually bothered them, but because it might seriously offend their social circle. I believed at the time that the Silbers' horror at my father's wishes to be cremated did not stem from a truly spiritual objection. It was an objection to how the Silbers felt they might be judged by others. I say "I believe," of course, because I will never truly know.

As an ever-evolving adult, I realize that in the exploration of my own Jewish identity, I could not then, nor shall I ever, fully grasp what it means to be a first-generation Ashkenazi Jew in America, especially one coming-of-age in the middle of the twentieth century. Being an Ashkenazi Jew in America is (still) a double-edged sword—we have the undisputed privilege of being able to pass as "white Europeans" and benefit from all that appearance entails, a benefit those of other races cannot employ when convenient. But still: Jews are always on guard. Jews have been persecuted, enslaved, oppressed, kicked-out, and systematically murdered for millennia, and still experience Anti-Semitism today.

All this, and then becoming thriving American adults raising children during the Holocaust? I can imagine being highly motivated—life-or-death motivated—to fully assimilate. This is still true today. I owe my grandparents a nod to that sociological complexity. I can disagree with their individual choices and overall behavior without that resentment being directed toward their Jewish identity. At eighteen, on that particularly terrible day, I was not a fully-realized expert on my family's connection to a cultural history fraught with persecution and genocide.

That day, in that room, all I cared about was my dead father and his final wishes.

Dad spent the last six months desperate to breathe, frantic about suffocating, and he didn't want to spend whatever concept of eternity he had buried beneath the earth in a box. He wanted freedom. And air. And a destruction of the body that he felt betrayed him. And all of that was fine by me. If God wanted to take it up with me, that would be just fine, thank you very much. I had a few more probing questions and choice words to take up with the Big Guy anyway. Just add this whole cremation business to the pile of minutia.

This funeral guy got it. He said to me privately that this actually happened all the time, the battle over the body. But they had cremated their fair share of Jews. It was the twenty-first century. *Just.*

"Sign here," he said, placing the papers with an exactness particular to people who choose to professionally deal with death. "And here."

My mother signed.

"Would you like to see Michael one last time?" he asked.

"No," Mom whispered.

With that, the screech was silenced—at least for the moment.

❦

When we returned home to 1367 Fairway Drive that night, the house had already taken on an eerie quality. It was still the house I knew—the walls, the carpets, the windows, the mementos were all the same—but it felt different. It felt off-center, like switching time zones as you drive through Indiana; like a zombie takeover where everyone looks the same but they could be a zombie; or like when you're on vacation and *Wheel of Fortune* and *Jeopardy!* come on television in reverse . . .

Or perhaps it was just that a soul was missing, a limb lost yet making its absence known.

Grey arrived that night.

Barukh atah Adonai Eloheinu Melekh ha'olam.[9]

---

9   *Blessed are you, Lord, our God, King of the universe.*

Grey

There are many images of my life that I will likely forget—the majority of which I think I shall be happy to—but one that is burned permanently into my memory is the way that Grey arrived on our doorstep that night.

Grey was toweringly tall, slim, and fair. He was also artistically bespectacled and wearing what he always wore in those days: slim jeans with long, pointed leather shoes, and a collared shirt below a fitted sweater of the finest material. He was an *aesthete*: a definitive appreciator of design, art, and beauty, and his clothing and personal appearance were no exception.

I remembered a bright full-mooned night Kent and I spent tucked within the security of darkness in one of a dozen or so hiding spots that we had collected as we courted in secret. The moon was luminous as it poured light on the large, open Opera Field, and everything beneath its sphere was glowing like a poem. There was Grey: walking briskly around the Opera Field's circumference discussing art and theater, planning the future of the art form with his roommate Michael Arden. Their hands painted the air about them with ideas, and their laughter filled the sky.

Grey loved the theater, as he still does, and he viewed design as his personal contribution to the theater he loved so well. "Some designers love geometry, architecture, fashion, shape, color. I love the theater," he would say.

By the end of the school year, Kent and Grey were best friends (I believe they were even MORP dates!), and they were always off together planning one thing or another, laughing hysterically, without a care in the world whether anyone understood why. The summer after graduation when we all worked at the summer camp (because we couldn't let go, let's face facts), Kent and Grey roomed together in the dormitory called Picasso House, and one could hear their laughter not only all across campus, but likely across the majority of the Midwest.

Hilarity aside, Grey was, in his way, the deepest of us all—his snobbery, haughtiness and all that inexhaustible laughter shielded the tenderest of hearts. He was sensitive, a Cancer (just like me—our birthdays are days apart), and one of my most important memories of the final days at Interlochen was holding Grey while he wept along the shores of Green Lake, his heart breaking from having to leave the only place that he—that any of us—had ever truly felt at home.

He had just driven up from Cincinnati where he was two months into his freshman year of college. Whether it was the news of the occasion, the drive, or an abysmal college experience that was wearing him down was unclear, but the normally flawless Grey looked like absolute shit.

"Hi," he said, "I parked in front."

"Fine," I replied. "Thanks for coming."

"Of course," he said, looking me right in the eye before giving me a brief hug. "So I'll get Felix to bring the bags in and we'll get started." Felix was his imaginary manservant, and that was going to be it for the emotions. We had work to do.

The three of us—Kent, Grey, and myself—immediately gathered in the kitchen, which we would eventually come to refer to as the Situation Room. We made more lists and charts, a calendar and a map, and devised a complex strategic plan worthy of most military war teams. The route to the airport. The route to each Greyhound station. Driving instructions. Accommodations. Funeral business. And defense strategy for familial drama. Three hours later, we had a plan—a streamlined, 453-point master plan.

Then we each grabbed our personal banana-sized cell phones, lifted the antennae,[10] and called everyone on our lists, walking in a circle, a finger in one ear as we collected the details. Our calls concluded and our phones went down like falling dominoes. In the silent room, we laughed. We were in a modern day Carol Burnett sketch—Molière meets *Frasier*, but with Greyhound stations and grumpy Jews.

With that task concluded, Grey went outside and made several trips back and forth to his black RAV4. Before long, he had brought in every last one of his belongings from Cincinnati. I think we all knew he was never going back. He moved into the downstairs room where he would remain for the next four months.

*   *

Of my central circle of friends, Lilly was the last to arrive.

She arranged a leave of absence, and caught a Greyhound bus up from Oberlin the following morning, arriving around lunchtime. She didn't arrive at the house until dinnertime, however, because despite our Black-Ops-worthy planning, we somehow forgot to pick her up. For three hours and 24 minutes—not that anyone was counting.

"I'm so sorry," Grey told her when he finally pulled up to get her. "I don't know how we missed you, Lil. We had everything planned down to the millisecond."

"It's OK," Lilly laughed. She was tired, but not even the tiniest bit irked. "I understand. I was just a little freaked out."

"Because you were a young woman alone in the Detroit Greyhound station? No worries there."

"Right," she said. Even her laugh was still sunny and Southern.

It would be the first of many identical journeys Lilly would take up the I-75, sometimes on the bus, but most often in her huge pale blue Dodge caravan, which made it look she was either dropping middle schoolers off at soccer camp or hauling a slightly "past-it" folk band to the latest

---

10   It was 2001, after all.

Renaissance Festival. Lilly would be the only one of us who would return to college at all—Grey and I would drop out of our programs, and Kent hadn't even gone in the first place. 1367 would become the place where all of us reassessed the next move. And joked about being college dropouts. Because, for the moment, we were.

Grey and Lilly finally pulled on to Fairway, and entered 1367.

"Hi," she said, meeting my gaze with her huge, hazel eyes, "I brought Oboe." Obviously Lilly was going to play at the funeral. Obviously.

"Come in," I said. And she did.

We arranged the sleeping situation. Grey and Kent would sleep downstairs in the lower guest room, which had previously doubled as my mom's design studio. It had its own bathroom, a dark window facing the River Rouge, and a trundle daybed we bought because I had seen one once on *The Price is Right* and thought the enthusiastic models made it appear outstanding. Lilly and I would share my room amid the fragmented souvenirs of a now forever-lost childhood. Mom felt understandably unenthusiastic about sleeping in the Bed of Death and thus took the spare bed in my dad's former office—an office he hadn't used in months as the disease took full control—where she'd remain for weeks.

Lil and I settled into my room. She put her bags down, pushed the hair off her weary face and sat next to me on the bed.

"Al?" she said.

"Yeah, Lil?"

The air was thick with swallowed tears and steadied nerves.

When she spoke again, her voice was quiet, but sure. "I've got this. We've got this."

"I know," I replied.

"You've got this."

"Thank you, Lilly."

She hugged me. That said it all. We immediately went downstairs and got to work.

There was an entire extended family of unhelpful people to play offense with. There were 7,000 people to pick up from Wayne County Airport, the Greyhound station (which we later discovered to be, in fact, three Greyhound stations, all sixteen miles apart). There were people to call, housing to arrange, people to feed. And oh yes: a funeral to plan.

And four eighteen-year-olds would do it all.

And so, as my dad's life ended, our life together as "the five of us" began.

Let Me Tell You About My Grandparents

Do you remember Grandpa Joe and the bed full of wonderful, adoring grandparents in *Willy Wonka and the Chocolate Factory*? Or Shirley MacLaine in *Terms of Endearment*? Or Peter Falk as the grandfather in *The Princess Bride*? Or Katharine Hepburn and Henry Fonda in *On Golden Pond*? These grandparents were perpetually bathed in afternoon sunlight, continually clad in earth tones, and all unendingly gentle as they spent time with their grandchildren in a fuzzy glow of adoration, charming life lessons and storytelling.

Well, my grandparents were just like that. Only instead of adoration, my grandparents offered something called "conditional love," and, instead of bedtime stories, I'd fall myself asleep not counting sheep, but counting what money was owed to whom, grudges, and grandma's pathological lies.

And, perhaps worst of all, there was not a scrap of chocolate. Because Grandpa Al didn't like chocolate, therefore no one else was allowed to like it either. And even if it was your birthday and you adored chocolate, even if you hated lemon cake with your whole being, even if you were *nine*: you got a lemon cake because "Grandpa doesn't like chocolate," and everyone is going to eat this lemon cake and enjoy it and that is the end of that because apparently dessert is not a democracy. That is why I hate yellow dessert to this very day (yes, including banana cream pie).

But other than that, they were just like those other grandparents. *Just* like.

( )

There we were, in the living room. First there was my grandmother Edna, inert. Then my grandfather Albert, staring straight ahead with an address book open in his lap. Next was yours truly, an oddly buoyant teenager under the circumstances. And then Mom, who was, at this point, an absolute puddle.

Rabbi Daniel Syme sat in the center before this line of ragged Silbers. He stared at us. Behind his glasses was a pair of dark, sensitive eyes set beneath a pair of bushy, expressive eyebrows. He was tall and impressive and wizened—emitting an immediate sense of sanity. I had no logical reason to, but I trusted him.

"So," he began, hands folded across his middle. "Tell me everything you can about Michael."

The rabbi needed to hear everything he could about Michael Silber in order to write a eulogy for this total stranger in forty-eight hours. This half hour was supposed to be ticking that box. So far it was profoundly sucking.

Well, there have been worse half hours. You know, in history.

( )

When I first told the story of the Teddy Bear House to a therapist, I told it with such theatrical gusto and panache, I was convinced I would be applauded, praised for my good humor in the face of madness, declared well adjusted, and be on my merry way. Turns out, in the wake of the tale, the very nice shrink responded with: "Right. I think we should meet *twice* a week."

It had happened the summer of 1992 when we were visiting my grandparents in their lakeside home in Metro Detroit. My grandmother Edna expressed an interest in spending a day with me, possibly later in the week.

"Just a grandma-granddaughter day," she said, the thought of which filled me with existential terror. Growing up as a quiet, contemplative and anxious only child, one comes to feel nervous about spending time alone with anyone that was remotely not your parents. Plus, my grandparents creeped me out. From the beginning—from the moment I was conscious enough to have instincts—I could tell something was fishy.

The day came. I settled into the front seat of her Oldsmobile, hair in long braids, dressed in purple leggings, and off we went to Farmington Hills.

Where were we going?

Why, that was a surprise!

To this day, I hate surprises.[11]

Classical music blared. After what felt like hours of driving through heavily wooded suburban territory—my grandmother's face peeking over the wheel while her tiny frame arched upward to see the road—we finally pulled into a parking lot. She stopped the car. We got out at a grocery store.

"This is the surprise, Grandma?" I asked.

"No, no, this is just a stop," she said, and in we went.

We picked up deli meats, a cake, vegetables cut into microscopic slices. Then we got back into the car, classical music blaring again, and we drove some more.

The long light of afternoon was cutting through the tops of the Michigan trees. We pulled onto a dirt road, turned a corner, and stopped before a tiny house sheltered by the wild brush and nearly void of daylight. It looked like every house in every fairy tale, where the little kid is about to be eaten.

"Is this the surprise, Grandma?" I said, my voice low.

"Yes," she said. "This is the Teddy Bear House!"

Now I had—and frankly still have—no idea what the "the Teddy Bear House" was or was supposed to be. All I knew was that I had never been more scared in my entire life and there was no way I was going in. I hoped

---

11   Almost as much as I hate yellow dessert.

my horror-struck expression was making this clear to Edna when she leaned down, informing me that, "The entire house is full of all kinds of teddy bears from all over the world! You will love it."

I would not.

She grabbed my hand and walked me up the forbidding path. As we headed toward the front stoop I heard the screeches of ominous birds, the squish of damp earth beneath my pink Keds, and as I began to imagine the kind of pie I would inevitably be cooked into, I suddenly loved and hated and missed my parents very, very much.

Edna knocked on the door. She knocked again. The silhouette of a similarly tiny old woman appeared and began unlocking about 200 dead-bolts before she finally opened the door a crack, saw that it was Edna, and opened it to reveal herself in full-on crazy lady regalia. If some people in life are weeds and others are flowers, this woman was a weed sprout-ing out of a bubblegum-pink kimono, with a thickly painted flower face, offset by Doris Day hair, and acrylic thorns.

"Come in, come in," she coaxed, singing it slightly, her giant eyelashes flapping. She escorted us into the house that was, as promised, covered floor-to-ceiling in teddy bears. They all looked as terrified as I was. *Per-haps*, their glassy eyes said silently to me, *perhaps if we stay very, very still she will spare us.*

"I was just making some tea. Would you like some, Edna?"

"No, thank you," Edna said. "I have to be going."

Going? I thought. *Thank God!*

"Sylvia is expecting me any minute and I can't be late for another of her get-togethers or she will absolutely never invite me again. I'm bring-ing extra goodies just to be sure she knows I mean business."

Who the hell is Sylvia? I thought. *And when do we leave?*

"Where are we going, Grandma?" I asked out loud.

"Oh no, dear," Edna replied, her voice going up an octave. "You are going to stay right here at the Teddy Bear House with this lovely lady while I go to a little party with my friends and then, later, I will come back and get you and it will all be our little secret."

I looked at Edna and felt my mouth drop open in astonishment. I panned across the room and slowly let my eyes settle on the Teddy Bear Woman, sitting on a dusty upholstered chair, hands entwined and head cocked like a young girl in an old fashioned painting, smiling so hard I was afraid her flower face might break apart.

I did not know how to call my parents. I did not know how to get help. I stared at her, too frightened to cry.

I spent the day helping the Teddy Bear Woman dust and organize, crawling into small spaces and cleaning little trinkets only a child's hands could properly get to, after she encouraged me to play the piano, sing and sit up straight, I was spent. I asked if I might lie down, which she allowed me to do after I finished assembling a dollhouse.

She led me upstairs to the top floor of the house, opened a tiny room with a key, and pointed to a small bed that must have once belonged to a child. This room was not covered in teddy bears—the only room in the house that wasn't. There was only a sole worn bear that lay on the bed itself. He looked tired. Broken. I sat down on the bed as I stroked his chest, then turned toward the door just in time to catch her locking me inside as she left.

I remained locked in that attic bedroom until Edna returned six hours later. I thanked the Teddy Bear Woman as best I could, ran to the car, and closed my eyes.

As we drove back, Edna asked me if I had had a nice day. I knew what she wanted me to say. I knew she was waiting for my lie. I would not give it to her. In an almost inaudible voice, I replied, "No."

Edna shifted in the driver's seat and the speed of the car increased. All bets were off now that Edna knew I could see right through her and that I had no regard for dishonesty or game playing. I was scaring her; children are supposed to be obedient, to fear the wrath of their elders. In this moment, I made it clear I would be doing neither.

Her voice transformed.

"If you ever tell your parents what happened today," she hissed, "I will be very angry."

"OK," I said. It was neither an agreement nor a disagreement. Merely a recognition.

We returned late that night. Both of my parents were waiting in the kitchen.

"How was your day?" Mom asked.

"Have a nice day o' fun with Grandma?" asked Dad with the voice of a carnival barker—he was an expert at manufactured enthusiasm.

"Great," I said. "Wasn't it, Grandma?" My eight-year-old eyes pierced her, unsmiling.

"Oh, yes," she said.

We both left the room, leaving my parents there, staring at one another in equal parts confusion and dread.

It took three days for Dad to get me to tell him what really happened the day of the Teddy Bear House. It was only because he reminded me that "secrets are important to honor, yes, but not when you feel afraid or are in danger. There is a sacredness in full honesty. Especially with yourself." He would know. For, as I was all too quickly coming to learn, my dad came from a family where nothing bonded you together like dark, horrible secrets.

When I later finished telling my father what had actually happened, I was in tears. The air went very still.

My father shook quietly in a righteous rage I had never witnessed in him before. He wrapped his arms around me, reassuring me I had done the right thing in telling him the truth, that what had transpired was scary, wrong and a "betrayal of trust," and the he was so sorry it had happened. Within the safety of his arms, warm and majestic as a lion's, I felt, I *believed*, that as long as I could remain right here, I would never be frightened again.

( )

I was engrossed in the memory of my father's embrace that day, strong around me as the realities unfolded. When I looked up, I saw that Rabbi

Syme had patiently walked through several rooms of our home, observing family photos guided by my mother, and skillfully dodged three teenagers zooming through the house at varying speeds.

Seated once again, we all sat there as Rabbi Syme took stock of the Silber Situation.

My grandmother Edna, steeped in *Overwhelm* (and rightly, for her son was dead), rocked back and forth in her chair, beating her breast, to, presumably, soothe herself.

"He was a professional baseball player," said grandma.

Oh dear. This was already going off course. My dad was not a professional baseball player (though he desperately wanted to be), and my grandmother's penchant for untruths was an indication of her inability to cope with reality. Of course I had empathy for my grandparents' loss, but in that moment my mind was tainted with memories of their prior human deficiencies. My grandmother was want to do this slow, rocking, breast-beating thing, and claimed that her failure to function was because she had "a Russian soul." Such was my father's initial tumor surgery when she rocked and wailed in the waiting room, and halfway through the eight-hour surgery took off to another part of the hospital claiming she had a piece of glass in her eye. Or when she "just couldn't" make it to dad's first chemotherapy treatment. Or when she didn't leave her bed for five years sometime in the mid-1950s due to a whispered-about depressive episode. All of these, I guess, because of the Soul. I had always pegged Russian souls to be a bit more stoic—beautiful, stark, and melancholic surging with an ocean of feeling alive just below the surface, churning to the tune of a tormented violin.

Or whatever. Apparently this Russian Soul was just incapable of behaving like an adult.

"And a member of Mensa," my grandfather grunted.

Not at all unlike cockroaches, for every one of my grandmother's flaws, there lay, waiting in the walls, a hundred more flaws belonging to my grandfather, lurking silently and carrying disease. This was, predictably, not a good start.

"Really?" the rabbi replied, scribbling it all down.

"No *not* really," I said, looking over at my grandfather, totally beyond tolerating this lie-fest for one more second. All bets were off now.

***

My father grew up wanting just two things from life: to play baseball and to have his father's love.

He loved baseball and played in high school, in college for the University of Michigan during undergrad, and after college he had to choose between Harvard Law School and playing first base for the Chicago White Sox.

But Albert had different plans for his eldest son. Albert was hard on Michael and expected his exceptionally bright son to become a lawyer and join the family business. Silber & Silber: Michael's name had practically been branded above the door since coming out of the womb.

Albert made it very clear that if Michael had any other plans for his life, he must rip them out by the roots, for if he did not join the business and accompany his father, Albert threatened to forsake him. Michael capitulated. It would be the first in a lifetime of compromises to earn his father's unwinnable approval.

Michael got his law degree from Harvard. Albert had gone to Wayne State University and the University of Michigan. Michael's second mistake was outshining the master.

When Michael returned home after law school, his name was already on the door, but Albert needed to take his son down a notch, to put him in his place after graduating from his fancy Ivy League institution at the top of his class. He made him do paralegal work below the qualifications of a man of his credentials—filing papers, driving to properties, getting coffee for clients. Michael took it all. He wanted his father to approve.

After two years of mind-numbing grunt work with no escape in sight, Michael hatched a plan: a merger of the most powerful law offices in

Detroit at the height of the city's power that would be successful for everyone involved. Crucially, it might also give Michael his freedom.

He worked on the plan for a year. Albert gave his blessing. Michael conceived of, plotted out, pitched, sold, and solidified the plan and, on the day everyone finally gathered together to sign the paperwork, Michael could hardly contain his excitement. *Freedom,* he thought, *freedom as well as my father's love and approval.* It could not have been a greater day.

Around the table went the legal contracts, each leader signing his name while praising the wunderkind who had made it all happen.

"Albert! Just look at your boy!"

"He's better than all of us, this kid is!"

At last, the papers fell before Albert.

Michael handed him the pen, eyes shining.

"Pop," he said, smiling. "I wanted to make you proud."

Albert looked at his son. He did not move.

"I never wanted this," Albert said, voice echoing. "I worked a lifetime to build this company and you sell it off like firewood?"

The realization dawned slowly upon Michael, working its way to his consciousness like a creeping acid. "Pop, please, you said—"

"Never mind what I said. The deal is off."

With that, Albert left the boardroom, leaving Michael there, sunk in a chair, to face the other men.

Michael stood and looked upon their faces—their expressions nearly as stunned as his own. He gathered the papers on the desk and he left the room, the office, Detroit, Michigan, and all that he had known. For all he knew, forever.

❨ ❩

I know, I know. I can hear you loud and clear reader: *Alright, Horatio Alger, we get it.* But Albert and Edna—these narcissistic, sad-sack loony tune Parents of the Year were not going to have custody of this narrative any longer. If they reigned supreme, if they controlled this moment with their money and their threats of withheld love, my father's humanity, his true character would die out with the dust he had already become.

I had to do something.

My mind—scorched by a kind of blinding clarity I had never known before or since—began to evaporate away any trace of the fog of grief, fear, or hesitation. I locked eyes with the rabbi and silently said to him: *Sir, it is very important that you listen to me. This is a man's eulogy we are talking about— his memory, his character, his imprint on the world. I cannot allow these bozos to tarnish his life any further. There is no room for family politics. Not in this funeral. Not if I have anything to say about it.*

The look he returned told me that he already knew it. He could see it all, but I would have to step up. So with that look, I began to talk.

I told him about gardenias. Their beautiful, pungent odor. That smell outside the duplex on Bedford Drive where we lived in Beverly Hills just before we moved to Detroit. Dad saw the way the sunlight hit them in the afternoon and, sparked by the word gardenia in the lyrics, sang "The Girl That I Marry" at the top of his lungs.

I told him about home movies and the way my father would always point, look directly into the camera and give his name, rank, and serial number. Or how he'd clown around, flipping fake burgers on a fake barbecue.

I told him about road trips to Mackinac Island and playing Yahtzee for hours during the dark skies and curfews of the LA Riots until I was too tired to be frightened. I told him about his black leather chair—the way it creaked in the office, how it smelled of leather and cologne, and how worn the arm rests were from all his countless hours of calculating and typing. I told him that my father loved baseball and theater and caramel corn and going to the library and the individual cherry pies you can get at the grocery store and eating yogurt with a very small spoon.

I told him about when my father took me to New York, where we went to my very first Broadway show—our family's favorite, *Ragtime*. I remembered when the lights came up for curtain call, tears were streaming down our faces, and we were silent, but he looked at me and his eyes told me: he knew that, one day, I would tell stories like that on Broadway stages.

I told him about the last night, when he had held my hand as though it were connected to my heart, and squeezed it urgently, so hard, that I thought my heart might break.

Is it possible to have someone else's life flash before your eyes? If so, that's what happened in that moment when I spoke so quickly and with such fervor that no one would ever have dared to speak over me. I couldn't stop. If I stopped talking, if I stopped chattering and laughing and vomiting anecdotes all over this warm-eyed holy man, I would lose a kind of battle that felt ripped from the pages of Sophocles. *Excuse me Antigone! Step aside Electra, I've got my own Greek tragedy to project to the back of the amphitheater of this Detroit living room.*

By the time I came to the end, I had stunned everyone—even myself.

"I think I see what is going on here," Rabbi Syme said after a long, considered pause. He unfolded his fingers and took a deep breath. "I am so sorry for your loss. All of you, I mean that. I am not aware of what your true beliefs are, or what you prescribe to in a holy way." He clutched at the sides of his chair and sat forward. "But I do know what I believe—I like to think that I have a special relationship with God, one I nurture and cultivate and deeply respect. And every once in a while, he gives me a crystal clear message that I feel obliged to listen to. And right now? He is telling me that this girl is supposed to give this eulogy in the temple on Friday. So, I am going to go with God on this one." He looked at me.

I was out of words. I simply nodded my acceptance.

My mother's eyes widened and looked from the rabbi to me, to my grandparents and back again. Albert was still boring a hole in the space directly before him, seething. Edna was a different matter altogether. She jumped up as if she had been Tasered, beside herself with anger and panic.

"She can't give the eulogy!" she exclaimed. "That ungrateful little *shiksa*[12] barely even knew him!" The air around her practically shook with her fury.

---

12   "Shiksa" is a derogatory Yiddish term for a non-Jewish girl or woman.

"Now," said the rabbi gently. "I am certain you don't mean that, Mrs. Silber."

The Rabbi was correct. Edna didn't actually mean *that*. Not exactly. What she really meant was that I would not perpetuate their version of the story, and if Albert had to endure his son's funeral not being about Albert, then the world might explode. It was clear that Edna had been instructed to keep things on track and things were going so far off-track—farther than anyone imagined—and this was about to be Family Politics Armageddon Twenty-first Century style because the fury of my love had pulled this lie-fest right out from under them. I had been given a gift by this unknown but very perceptive rabbi, and I had not only stolen the eulogy, I had stolen their thunder, and that made my thunder grow stronger. (Because, that's how it works, right? Like *Highlander*? There can be only one?)

"She is going to ruin everything!" my grandmother screeched, tearing at her hair in desperation.

Everything? I thought to myself, rolling my eyes. *Also, I'm going to need that "World's Best Grandma" mug back.*

But what I actually said was, "I think you've made your point, Grandma."

I had won.

Now I just needed to write a eulogy.

Kinko's

(*At rise: Kent and Lilly enter a local twenty-four-hour Kinko's on Detroit's legendary eight-laned promenade dotted nowadays by steak houses, furniture warehouses, and vintage ice-cream joints, Woodward Avenue. It is 1 a.m. The funeral is tomorrow. No one has slept in over a day. The funeral program must be printed. When, lo! The typical middle-of-the-night college-aged functionary approaches.*)

KINKO'S GUY: Hi
LILLY: Hi there we w—
KG: Hey.

(*There is a very awkward pause.*)

LILLY: Heeeey—
KG: Welcome to Kinko's.
LILLY: Thanks?
KG: How can I help you?

LILLY: We need some copies.
KG: Yeah.

(Lilly looks to Kent. He smiles. She looks back at the Kinko's Guy who is cleaning out some scum from under his fingernail.)

   LILLY: Is there any world in which I could go back there and do this myself?
   KG: No.
   LILLY: Right. So . . . *(she digs into her bag for the funeral program)* we would like this *(she presents it)* to be printed on this *(she presents it)* stone-colored card stock. Two programs per sheet. Centered.

(The Kinko's Guy stares at her.)

   KG: Centered?
   LILLY: Yes. Centered.
   KG: Like, in the middle?
   LILLY: Yes.

(The Kinko's Guy stares at her.)

   LILLY: Please?

(The Kinko's Guy takes the sheet.)

   KG: OK. How many do you want?
   LILLY: One hundred sheets.
   KG: Cool. Gimme a sec.

(Kent and Lilly take a seat. It is 1:12 a.m. and clearly this poor local kid is only there to vaguely prevent the copy machines from being stolen, the vandals of Metro Detroit from Xeroxing their ass, their face, or, God forbid, copyrighted material.)

   KG: Here you go.

LILLY: Wow, that was fast!

(*Lilly and Kent look down and behold the Guy's handiwork. It is not in the center.*)

LILLY: I am so sorry, but you see, it is not actually centered.
KG: Oh, wait—you wanted it like in the very center?
LILLY: (*Tensely*) Yes.
KG: Do you want me to do it again?
LILLY: Yes, please.
KG: OK, gimme a sec.

(*Lilly looks to Kent who looks back with a similar look of disbelief and despair.*)

KG: (*returning*) OK, here we go!
LILLY: (*looking at the page*) No.
KG: No?
LILLY: No. You see, now it is indeed, in the center, but the text is on an angle. It is not straight.
KG: But it is centered?
LILLY: Yes.

(*And it occurs to her: This youth does not care about their deadline. This youth does not understand that someone is dead. This youth cares more about smoking weed and hanging out in the many illustrious parking lots of Birmingham, Royal Oak, and Troy, of driving from 7-Eleven to A&W and back again with some Midwestern Christmas-Trees-and-Corn Queen.*)

KG: I thought you wanted it in the center.
LILLY: Yes.
KG: And it is in the center. I don't—
KENT: I think what we are trying to express—

(Kent interrupts what is certain to be Lilly's moment of self-combustion with what we shall later learn to be his signature tone of patient, polite condescension that he utilizes in moments such as these: when dealing with imbeciles, unfair people, and when ordering food from a menu that has ridiculous names. Here that voice is—at what was now approaching 1:43 a.m.)

— is that we would like the text to be both straight *as well* as in the center of the sheet. Do you see? Our concern here is that this copy is straight, but not in the center. This one is centered, but not straight. We would like the next one to come out of your copy machine both in the center *and* straight. Does that make sense?

KG: Totally.

KENT: Great. Let's give this one more try.

(The Kinko's Guy returns again. Lilly cannot even look. She keeps her eyes held on Kent who looks down and keeps a cool demeanor as he realizes that it is still wrong. All wrong. He takes a breath and places his hand over it, eyes intent on Lilly.)

LILLY: Skip the part that is going to make me nuts.

KENT: That would be all of it. *(He looks at Kinko's Guy again)* Try again please.

(The Kinko's Guy walks away, and does. When he returns? Victory. Well, minor victory— it still looks pretty bad but it is both centered as well as straight and, at 2 a.m., they will take it.)

KENT: One hundred sheets of that, please.

(Lilly and Kent glide back down a desolate Woodward Avenue toward 1367. In Xerox harmony, they pray that Al has written a brilliant eulogy in their absence, and that sleep is in their future. They are silent—the first silence they've had since the chaos began, and the last until it is over.)

Writing the Eulogy

I was holding an apple. There is a very specific way my father always went about eating apples. The steps taken were as follows:

1. Select the apple (preferably a Fuji, Red Delicious, or Braeburn)

2. Remove the insidious fruit sticker

3. Curl that stupid sticker into a ball and either:

    a. dispose of it properly,

    b. flick it into the ether, or

    c. stick it somewhere else equally, if not entirely more inappropriately, irritating for the sake of both comic irony and convenience.

4. Carefully select the perfect first bite, preferably in the top "breast" of the apple. (Beginning well is key.)

5. Break the skin with your teeth, biting with full force while sucking the juice and assessing the quality of this apple experience based on overall flavor, sweetness, juiciness, texture, mealiness and, above all, crispness and "crack."

6. Continue to eat from the top to the bottom of the apple in large bites until nothing remains but the core.

7. Lick fingers, switch hands, repeat.

8. Eat bottom of the apple including bottom stem and half of the core, then the core itself, then the top of the apple.

9. Then, holding the stem, clean it off like meat from a bone in an old cartoon.

10. Contemplate the apple stem you are left holding in your hand.

11. Finish the procedure by placing the remaining stem in an inappropriate or annoying place that is not the garbage.

I had not realized it until that very moment, but that was exactly how I also eat an apple.

I had procured the apple in my hands from the my family's storage of food that had been in the fridge before he was dead. This apple was not a part of the donations, the deli platters, the tiny, soldiered sticks of vegetables that came with dips and spreads and soup, and enough bagels to stuff a mattress. It had been there before he died, and now I was about to eat his apple—or an apple that could have been his, had he lived.

The apple was old and the skin wrinkled when I pinched it. As I took the first bite, I discovered the sweetness to be gone, the fruit mealy. Oh well. Nothing can be fresh forever.

But I kept eating the not-fresh apple—breaking the skin, sucking the juice, passing judgments, licking fingers, following the steps. I concentrated on eating the apple because I could not do what needed to be done.

When they had gotten back from Kinko's, Kent and Lilly had sat me down on the bed in my childhood bedroom. I had changed back into the same pajamas I was wearing when he died. They opened Kent's laptop, a Mac from the late nineties that was the same teal color as my pajamas.

I sat on the bed, my hands resting limply on top of my crossed legs. I made bad jokes to put them at ease, but they were not laughing. There was not time. It was well after midnight and the funeral was in less than ten hours, and there was no eulogy because I had not, would not, could not write it.

So Kent and Lilly almost held me down. Their faces were tired; their hands extended toward me as if to press the magnitude upon me through their gestures, as if their hands might keep me from toppling like a crumbling tower. They made it clear that this was it—there was no more procrastinating to do.

They opened the laptop, they handed me the apple, and they closed the door.

Whether or not I wanted to write it, the eulogy had to be written.

Thirty minutes went by. I did not move. I stared at the closed door, and I ate the apple. It took me biting the outside of my hand to jolt me from the trance and look down into the palm: just the stem.

I closed my eyes and began.

I am at Mackinac Island—a tiny island off the coast of Northern Michigan between the Upper and Lower Peninsulas. Idyllic. Iconic. A summer haven for migrating travelers. We had just convinced ourselves to permanently set roots down in Michigan after spending the entire summer there with my grandparents in 1993. It is all settled; we will move the following December, pack our entire Californian life up in boxes, and the Silber family will cross the country and live. Such decisions are harrowing, but so are entire summers spent with your strange grandparents, thus we are exhausted and in need of a drive. A long one. We took the I-75 up the west coast of Michigan, through Traverse City and up toward the Mackinac Bridge, then over it onto the Island. It is magical—a dot of land that time has forgotten. No cars, only horses, bicycles, and carriages. The sun is blaring, the lake water is glistening, and all of us are so happy. We take the tour, behold the grandeur; we waltz in and out of the quaint little shops and taste the local specialties, Mackinac Island Fudge and its ice cream. We sit on a bench and take photos and I note, as I nestle next to my father, that I fit perfectly in the crook of his strong and effortlessly elegant arm that is curled around me. I hold an ice cream cone. My face hurts from smiling. This will be the final family memory I have of the three of us before Dad's illness began. I am eight years old and completely in love with my family, with being alive and in the world. An entire day is spent together. Without worry. Joyfully.

I am on the Opera Field with Kent. It is late; only half an hour remains before we are both supposed to sign in at our dorms, but the stars are so bright and we are hiding in a shed curled around one another, unable to get close enough, in the desperate, swollen manner that only two seventeen-year-olds in the first flushes of true love in the springtime can possess.

I am in Los Angeles and I am four years old. We are still at Century Hill, just outside Studio City, living in my first home. A giant box of Barbie dolls lies beside me, and my dad is there, looking dapper in his business suit, fully engaged in playing with me. He is dressing the dolls and organizing the clothing and asking me a thousand questions, all of which he appears to be genuinely interested in. This would be a quality I would come to recognize as uniquely his, and not at all unusual, in the years to come. We have hit an impasse at clothing organization because the Barbie clothing hangers have gone missing. Now we are both pawing the bottom of the box in an attempt to retrieve them—all attempts, thus far, in vain. At long last, my tiny hand clutches one and lifts it triumphantly to the surface. I am beaming and my dad raises both hands in the air as if I had scored a goal. "Perseverance!" he exclaims, and I raise my hands up too, wanting to be just like him. "Perseverance!" I repeat, not knowing what it means, but knowing it is good.

I am in the car three months ago—three months before my father's death. It is just after my birthday in July. My parents have come up to Interlochen to visit and I am driving alone in the car with Dad, who is incoherent. He coughs, and large chunks of bloody tissue fly from within him into a handkerchief he has handy for this express purpose. The handkerchief is dark black with blood. I am filled with horror as I continue to drive, eyes not on the road, but on the handkerchief. He draws my gaze up as he comes up for air. The moment is very still, and we make a silent agreement not to talk about it.

It is a Sunday morning in the past. I only know it is Sunday because the house is full of the aroma of bagels from Elaine's on Rochester Road. We're gathered around them, so fluffy and full there is not even a hole in the center.

It is Shabbat, and at Temple Isaiah (my Jewish preschool in Los Angeles) every Shabbat they select an "*Aba*" and an "*Ima*" ("father" and "mother" in Hebrew) for that week's celebration to teach the young children about leading services. This week I am the *Ima*, and Dad and I have gone downtown to the Jewish bakery and bought two fluffy *challah* breads for the occasion— one for me (to hold on top of my head during the preschool ceremony that will take place at tiny desks above a sea of blocks and dress-up clothes and colorful plastic chairs) and an extra for later that evening. Dad is smartly dressed in a suit and overcoat to accompany me to preschool Shabbat, and, as we approach the school hand-in-hand, we stop at the abandoned cinema a few addresses down from the school. Dad spots the same homeless man that has sat upon the honey-colored steps every day for as long as I can recall. Dad stops before him and says, "Hello," my little hand clutched in his. He hands the man the second challah bread, smiles and says, "Have a great weekend, OK?" The homeless man looks up at my dad and grins, smelling the loaf and laughing out loud with utter joy. I look over my shoulder as we walk away to watch him take his first bite.

I am fifteen and A, S, and K—three seemingly innocuous older girls who at one time I thought to be my friends—are making my life very difficult. They are all two years older, each killing me in their own ways, sometimes together, sometimes apart. Silence. Rumors. I don't know what I have done to upset them other than receive leading roles in the school play before what they deemed to be "my time." Perhaps they felt it was unfair. Perhaps it was. It didn't feel unfair; I was as talented and as hard-working as anyone, but perhaps it was unfair to get the lead so young. I am wearing a dark-gray peacoat as I do at all times. I cannot move. I am curled in my bed. I have been sleepwalking through my life for months, unable to smile, or laugh or focus on schoolwork. All of this, and Dad is sick—so sick—and no one is talking about it, therefore I feel I have no right to talk about it either. The truth is I do not feel safe anywhere. All I ever feel is the worst kind of fear—cold, quiet, invisible, and unmentioned. The safest place is inside this gray peacoat that I will not take off for a year.

I am upstairs doing homework on the weekend, and the University of Michigan has just scored and the entire house is shaking from the volume on the downstairs television being turned up full blast as the Michigan fight song blares. "Hail to the Victors." Mom and I make our way downstairs and observe Dad as he marches around in sharp turns (the way one might in a marching band), stone faced, and holding an invisible cat in his hands as he does so. To anyone else this would be an odd sight, but not to Mom and I who are used to it. This old tradition used to contain a real cat, a cat my parents owned just before I was born named Pounce, who was always ready and willing to march whenever Michigan scored. Now he is only there in spirit.

I am in the Traverse City Emergency Room an hour after Dad has collapsed during the final few days of performances (known as Festival) at Interlochen. It is two days before my high school graduation. Kent kissed me goodbye at the school infirmary where I heard the news before I left for the hospital. He held me close and watched with a different kind of love than I had ever seen in his face as I drove away. When I arrive, our family friends David and Robin are already here. They both stand by his bedside and Robin holds my hand. "Things are different now," she whispers in her soothing voice as she strokes my back. I stare at her hard because I don't understand what she means. I understand it now. Dad is doing that thing where he sings everything subtly off-key until someone notices. He is doing this to be funny.

It is.

I am sitting by his bedside the morning after his death. I see that one of his eyes is a little bit more open than the other, and I am too scared to close it. I stare at him and it is clear that this death was not peaceful, nor was it particularly welcome. It was painful and slow and it is written all over his unrecognizable face. Filled with an oddly sterile kind of calm, I sit there, wishing there was some kind of manual to follow, a list of to-dos that didn't make me feel like I was in a movie or a nightmare or some odd combination of both. I don't know what to do, but I want to mark the moment somehow, so I begin to sing a song from my favorite musical that will, without question, continue to haunt me for the rest of my life.

Dad is singing a made-up song that resembles a well-known standard, but is not, because he is changing all of the words. He is changing all of the words to amuse himself and others, but mostly himself, and the enthusiasm grows as he sings. It is making me crazy, and finally I crack. "Dad!" I yell, eyes wild. "Chill, Al," he says, eyes closed and snapping Ray Charles style, "It's just *scat* . . . "

We are "messing" on a Saturday afternoon. "Messing" is our term for weekend adventures that didn't include big plans. Messing is like window shopping—fun, noncommittal, and all about the journey and who you spend it with. Today we are in the car playing a game we like to call "Twenty Turns," which is exactly what it says on the label—you get in the car ripe for adventure and, at each intersection, choose between right, left or straight ahead, and after twenty of those, you find something fun to do wherever you end up. It is a perfect Michigan summer day, and we end up at the batting cages where he teaches me to switch hit. Then off to a mini-golf course. By dusk, we end up in the middle of nowhere at a firework warehouse and return home with a car full of patriotic red, white, and kablooey, which we set off in the park down the street from 1367 after we get home.

It is 1991, Los Angeles in a flash flood. My second-grade class is downtown seeing *Wind in the Willows*. Just before we head inside, it begins to rain. When we leave, the streets are like raging rivers and our car is halfway under water. Dad trudges through, pushes the car out from the water, manages to get the ignition started, and leaves the car in park in the middle of the road before he lifts the four little girls from the mound of grass far above the curb over the high water, and into the safety of the car. My dad is a hero.

I am fifteen and in the dark-gray peacoat. Dad comes into my room and sits down, explaining that he won't be able to come to my school play. I am playing Annie Sullivan in *The Miracle Worker,* and A, S, and K are the other leads and they have never hated me more. I want to quit. They want me to quit. But Annie Sullivan would not quit, so I do not. I am devastated by A, S, and K, and I am devastated that Dad cannot make the play. But I am mostly devastated because Dad is having surgery. Because Dad has cancer. Again. I do not tell A, S, and K. I do not tell my teachers, I do not tell anyone. No one will sympathize, no one will care or show compassion—teenagers only care about themselves and parents only care about their children and teachers only care about their tenure—and so I do not tell anyone. I actually believe that these girls would be delighted by my devastation and most likely use it to hurt my family even more, and I can handle them hurting me but if they attack my hurting family I cannot be responsible for my reaction. Dad finishes explaining and adds that he will be there in his heart— "just like Danny Kaye in Hans Christian Andersen, when he gets locked in the closet by the ballet master and misses the entire performance. Remember what he said to the ballerina he loved so much when they released him the next day? 'But I was there—I heard the music and could see every moment of your performance in my mind.' It will be just like that." My eyes leak though my face is immovable. I nod. I hug him. I hate cancer.

It is bedtime and we are finishing *The Magician's Nephew*.[13] Dad and I have read all of the Chronicles of Narnia together, and he tells me that tomorrow we can finish the final book and isn't that exciting? I start to cry a little and tell him I want to hold off on starting the final book. "But don't you want to know how it ends?" he asks. "I know how it ends," I whisper, my head resting on his chest. I do. And I don't want it to be over just yet.

We are in the car driving up to Interlochen in the fall of 1998. We are driving up just the two of us to check out the year-long Academy. This trip is just before he is rediagnosed. Just before the real trouble begins for me at my current school. We are in the car, about to pull into Cadillac, and listening to the cast recording of *Ragtime*. While stopping at a gas station, the intro to the "New Music" number begins and Dad, in typical Dad fashion, changes the script ever so slightly. Creating what would become a classic family line, he speaks over Brian Stokes Mitchell with a straight face: "This is called... *Ragtune*."

I am backstage at Interlochen. It is my senior year, and I am playing the role I have dreamed of playing all summer—Amalia Balash in *She Loves Me*. It is opening night, and I have not yet made my entrance, so I am sneaking a peek at my dad's face as he watches my teacher David sing "Days Gone By." Dad is sitting in the same seat he always chooses at the Harvey Theatre—the last row in the center section, on the right hand aisle. I can see his face as plain as anything, lit from both the stage and from within. His smile is so broad and genuine, and he is swaying along with the music so full of unharnessed joy I wouldn't be surprised if he ran down the aisle and joined David in song. He has never been happier

---

13   We read the Narnia books in the original release order, in which *The Magician's Nephew* is the penultimate book.

to be anywhere and I can see it on his face as I observe him, unaware. I know that I will never forget the expression on his face in this moment as long as I live.

I am in my room and it is the morning of the funeral.

I look down at the computer. The eulogy has been completed. It glows upon the screen in front of me.

PART TWO: FUNERAL!

Love Keeps Going

There was a period of time in 2010 when I lived with Tyne Daly. I know what that sentence sounds like and—just to anticipate all of your questions—yes, it was everything you thought and imagined and hoped it would be. She's both a classy broad and a true lady, an old soul who can play like a child with a sharp-as-cheddar mind and the best legs I've ever seen. Anyway, in 2010 I was not certain in what city, or which country, I was living exactly, but in May of that year all I knew what that I was living with Tyne Daly.

We had recently completed the production of Terrence McNally's *Master Class* in Washington, DC, at the Kennedy Center. It was the play that would, the following year, be my Broadway debut. In a minor panic about what the heck to do with my life at that somewhat pivotal moment, Tyne suggest I stay in New York and temporarily set up camp in her New York apartment.[14]

While that could all likely be a memoir of its own, this story isn't really about the—admittedly wonderful—Tyne. It just takes place in her apartment.

Tyne did not have a television set, but someone had given her a small-screen DVD player. In my first few weeks settling in to my New York City

---

14   As one does.

existence, I would watch classic films late into the night. On May 21, 2010, I watched *Shakespeare in Love*.

I had seen the movie before, but until that night, I feel I had never *truly* seen it. When it had come out in 1998, I had been fifteen—already a great lover of theater, but unfamiliar with many of the British actors who graced the screen—a few of whom would someday become my friends and colleagues. I could not fully appreciate many of the factual nods, inside jokes, and delightful wordplay that peppers the incredible screenplay, nor was I as appreciative about the natures of both creativity and love itself as I would grow to become. I was still a teenager. I liked the film, it was about everything I enjoyed, but I did not "get" it until that night in Tyne's apartment.

Dad had really loved this film. It took a lot to get him to focus on television for an extended period without his restless and brilliant mind wandering to the flood of ideas that constantly came to him. But this film? He adored it. He had watched it over and over again, sometimes late at night by himself. Something about its message moved him, made him believe in something. And on May 21, 2010, I finally understood *why*: true love and the theater, and the transformative power of both. That the once-undignified artists are revealed to be the greatest contributors to society's spiritual nobility. As the character of James Burbage says directly to Shakespeare in the film:

"We must show them that we are men of parts . . ."

Men of many roles, facets, identities, and chapters. Men of potential. Men of character.

It was so curious—adult Al profoundly connecting with adult Dad, in the present, in real time. So absolute was the understanding, so acute was this moment of connection, I actually picked up the phone and began to dial my old phone number to call him and share. It felt so powerfully for a brief moment like he was still here. In fact, this experience of connecting with my father in that moment is proof that, in so many ways, he still *is* here.

And on that day, alone in a beautiful apartment on the island of Manhattan, I looked briefly out at the sky and put my phone down. I smiled.

I had learned something important about loss: Love keeps going.

The Protagonist Wishes to Reiterate Her Feelings toward Her Grandparents without Overdoing It

```
M  Y  O  S  T  F  A  M  I  M  Y  L  N  I  D
D  L  E  S  A  R  E  S  A  O  E  M  O  E  E
E  R  W  H  R  A  T  N  C  R  N  A  I  Z  L
T  E  Y  B  E  U  I  S  T  W  R  E  S  A  U
R  S  R  E  B  A  R  E  X  T  O  R  S  A  S
O  I  H  T  L  A  E  H  L  A  T  N  E  M  I
I  M  S  U  I  P  E  R  K  I  T  N  R  C  O
T  D  O  L  S  F  C  R  U  E  A  L  P  R  N
W  I  T  H  H  O  L  D  I  N  G  A  P  O  A
N  L  O  R  T  N  O  C  D  U  N  U  O  O  L
L  A  C  I  G  O  L  O  H  T  A  P  S  K  U
M  S  I  S  S  I  C  R  A  N  A  L  L  E  E
V  E  M  I  C  H  I  G  A  N  L  O  F  D  I
N  S  A  T  I  E  C  N  O  C  Y  E  N  O  M
N  E  Z  J  W  A  G  P  I  O  U  X  O  F  U[15]
```

---

15 Hidden Message: "Most families are somewhat crazy but we are an extra super kind of cruel and unusual level of insane."

Funeral: A How-to Guide

Funerals are a social mystery. A formulaic social mystery, but mysterious nonetheless, for the sporadic nature of funerals, mixed with a general avoidance of discussion on the subject in Western culture, makes it difficult to acquaint oneself with what's expected in terms of proper behavior. You just muddle through each funeral, hoping you're doing the right thing, and then you largely forget about it until you have to muddle through it again the next time.

Here are a few basics to keep in mind.

First, it is essential to make certain you are at a funeral. How, you ask? There will be signs—not literal signs, mind you, not neon signs in childlike scrawl stapled to the side of trees and lampposts as if the funeral were some kind of macabre yard sale—but more subtle indicators. Someone should be deceased. (Make certain someone is, or else you are not at a funeral, you are at a very dark house party. Someone being dead is often the point of the funeral, differentiating it from any other kind of social function.) There will also be a somber mood, unless you are cynical, or Irish, or you are at the funeral of a particularly Wicked Witch.

Also, make certain that you are at least within Six-Degrees-of-Kevin-Bacon away from the deceased. You might not know the deceased personally, but make certain that you are doing more than merely being there for the free deli spread. That would make you a funeral crasher.

Which brings me to an important point: Do not—either consciously or unconsciously—crash a funeral. The very worst kind of crasher is on a par with the evilest of evil, e.g. Sauron, both the Alien and the Predator, and Hitler.

Funeral etiquette is tricky. As previously mentioned, it is an unpleasant subject to dwell upon and, unless you are in public service or are Lord Voldemort, your experiences with funerals may tend to be few and far between. There are a few things to keep in mind.

First, food. During the days immediately following a death, the family of the deceased is usually too overwhelmed to carry on the normal every-day chores, such as cooking and cleaning. So food would be more than welcome, unless:

a. It is somewhat preposterous food,

b. You bring steak sliders to a vegan household,

c. Everyone brings the exact same dish, or

d. The family's fridge gets so packed with so many containers of soup and pasta and goulash that it threatens to explode.

Make certain you mark your Tupperware and list any cooking instructions. Then, once in attendance of the funeral, make certain you eat both a giant and a finger sandwich. Science says the smaller or larger you make a sandwich, the more awesome it becomes.

You will likely see people you have not seen in years. For better or for worse. This is not the time to confront the man who slept with your ex-husband. A certain degree of flirting with hot strangers depends on how close you are to the deceased or their family.

Subdued colors are most appropriate for funerals. Do not wear a costume or a veil. Please. This isn't a Brontë novel.

Simple, brief expressions of sympathy are usually best. Remember, above all, you are attending the funeral to show respect for the person who has recently passed away, and your role is to support the survivors. This is not your platform for venting past disagreements, collecting on debts, or hitting on the widow. Also, avoid at all costs making grieving a contest. People who think grief is a contest are instant losers of said contest. Don't back a horse in that race.

Cause of death can be a difficult subject, and should therefore be avoided. Try to avoid statements such as "I am so sorry to hear of the loss of Nathan's head—I am certain once they trawl the landfill for it, they can return it to the funeral home and you can finally have your peace." Not *piece*—avoid those terrible puns. Just say, "I'm sorry for your loss." Sending flowers is also a traditional way to express your condolences. Be aware however, that if the grieving family is particularly poetic, flowers that will eventually die in about a week only serve as a reminder that everything dies. Just like their dead family member.

Sometimes things do not go as planned. If, throughout the course of the funeral process, you discover that the funeral home has, say, accidentally kept the body in a ball pit or cremated the incorrect corpse or anything else classified as a "disaster," by all means keep that intel to yourself. It is safe to say that today is already pretty shitty for the family of the deceased. Thus that info can wait.

Trust that in time it will all just seem like most episodes of *Three's Company* that feature the Ropers—hysterically macabre.

Keep these points in mind and you should be fine. If you screw up, you've blown it—absolutely feel free to bludgeon yourself to death with your own unwanted flowers. But before you do, just make certain no one screws up as royally at your funeral.

Funeral-ku

1.
No more soup. Hate soup.
Tupperware shoved tight in the
refrigerator.

2.
Teenagers in charge.
Mandatory yarmulke.
Cancer is a bitch.

3.
"Ashes to ashes"
is tradition. I suggest
"Disgust to disgust."

Funeral: Prologue to a Farce

(*Lights up on a bare stage. MIKE, the STAGE MANAGER, wears a cap and sits by the gathered stage curtain. He is reading a newspaper. It is only after a moment that he looks out over the stalls, nods, then puts down his paper and moves to the very back wall, which is concealed in almost total darkness. Within an instant we hear him pushing a large structure forward and locking it in place. And we see it: across the stage we now see four doors. The STAGE MANAGER makes his way around to the front and knocks on each door on his way to the microphone, downstage left when suddenly—*)

KENT: Mike!

(*KENT pops his head around the side of the door set structure, anxious. MIKE halts and turns around with lukewarm enthusiasm.*)

KENT: Mike? Hi. We were wondering back here if we are going to be running the whole thing?

(*MIKE looks out across the stalls for the answer. Turns back. Nods.*)

KENT: OK, because I have a cast of people back here that are not entirely off book or certain of the blocking or—

GREY: *(appearing)* And some of us, though remarkable to believe it, are not actually actors!

LILLY: *(appearing)* Yeah!

(Door 2 opens and a handful of people, all holding scripts and various props, spill out.)

PERSON 1: Kent, what is going on?

PERSON 2: I am not going to be playing all of the old people, not again! Not after what I went through trying to create a really believable Old Adam in *As You Like It* last spring.

PERSON 3: Honey, please.

PERSON 2: No! I'm tired of it. All I ever play is the old people. I'm done. Let me play a crazy neighbor or something.

PERSON 3: Someone make him shut up.

KENT: I see his point. *(Turns to PERSON 2.)* Would you be willing to play one old person? *(He searches the character lexicon.)* "Grandpa Albert's business partner Norm Katzenblat" as well as "The Husband in the Neighbors Who Moved Away in '98?"

PERSON 2: Deal.

(More PEOPLE begin to swamp the stage from the wings.)

PERSON 4: Wait! If he gets to pick his part, then I want another part too! I don't want to just play myself if I can play a crazy cousin or something.

PERSON 5: Come on. We don't have time for this.

PERSON 6: Kent, do I have to wear this costume? It constricts . . . I can't give what I want to give—

KENT: OK, look. *(To PERSON 4)* You can play "Conservative Woman Next Door." *(To PERSON 5)* And you can play "Her Husband." *(To PERSON 6)* And you can wear anything you want. In fact, go look out in the garage where Cathy keeps all her costumes in order of time period. I'm sure you can find what you're looking for. Everybody set?

(*A throng of PEOPLE come teeming up the center aisle of the theater.*)

>   **PERSON 7:** Not yet, Kent!
>   **KENT:** Where did all of you come from?
>   **PERSON 8:** We just got in from Interlochen.
>   **KENT.** When?
>   **PERSON 8:** Just now.

(*Enter the ADULTS: Theater teachers and husband and wife, DAVID and ROBIN.*)

>   **NEIL:** David! (*He looks to Kent.*) Oh Kent, now that David is here can
>   he play the old people?
>   **GREY:** Neil! Kent and I are playing Al's *grandparents* for God's sake, get
>   a grip.

(*MICHAEL ARDEN enters from the wings in a suit, sheet music spilling from his arms.*)

>   **MICHAEL:** Kent, where is my accompanist? If we are doing a full run I
>   need a piano, I'm not singing the funeral number without music!
>   **LILLY:** Good point!
>   **CROWD:** KENT!

(*Bedlam. EVERYONE begins talking at once, crowding both KENT and the stage with their protestations. Then, after a moment, a loud, piercing whistle stops the action flat. It is MIKE, The STAGE MANAGER, who is taking HIS fingers out of mouth, staring at all of them with the first expression we have seen from HIM yet—pure amusement. HE points to the back of the theater, to whomever HE has been nodding to, and EVERYONE looks in turn, trying to make out a figure from the darkness.*)

Suddenly, a VOICE booms from the theater's speaker system, known in theatrical vernacular as the "God mic.")

AL: Hello everybody.

(KENT *bursts downstage center, the character lexicon and Show Bible in his arms, his face desperate.*)

KENT: Al! Please sort this out.
GREY: Yes, we're dying up here!
KENT: None of us know what to do.
AL: (*her voice coming from the God mic*) No.
(*PAUSE.*)
KENT: What do you mean 'no'?!
AL: I can't help you. Not this time. This time, I need all of you to
      help *me*.

(EVERYONE *looks at one another awkwardly. Blinks. Nods. Resolve. EVERYONE agrees to do their best with the mess they've all been left in . . .*)

LILLY: (*nodding*) OK.
JESSICA: Yeah. You got it.
KENT: Alright people, you all heard her—places please.

(EVERYONE *moves. Props are placed, jackets decided upon, vocalizing done, crossing and recrossing. Then at last, everyone settles. We're going to grit our teeth and pray.*)

🦶 🦶

But that, of course, wasn't how it happened.

Instead, on the morning of the funeral—Friday, October 12, 2001—I pressed the snooze button before finally waking at 7 a.m. in a puddle of my own drool with my hair three times the size it had been yesterday, having apparently grown over my face like the evil vines in *Sleeping*

Beauty. On the screen of Kent's laptop in front of me, I stared at a eulogy I barely remembered writing. And I was suddenly aware that, in a few hours, the tone of the day would be entirely up to me. My dad would either be mourned or celebrated.

Last night, everyone had arrived from everywhere. Lord knows where they were staying.

I dashed downstairs in my frightening state and printed the eulogy. It was microscopic.

I increased the font size and printed again.

Ink was low. Plus, now the eulogy was fourteen pages long.

Shit.

Lilly and Kent were already up, cell phones duct-taped to their ears. Grey had spent the night at the Hausers, where the Interlochen contingent had (apparently) spent the night in their giant basement, and was already on the other end of Kent's cell phone.

"Grey," Kent warned on this, exactly one month after September 11, "you be very careful out there today, we're on Terror Alert. This is full-out-no-marking Code Orange."

"I know," Grey said. "I know that. It means something might go down somewhere in someway at some point in time." Because we were all dealing with death, too, without the honor of myopically focused news coverage, we felt we had the right to be this snarky. What other choice remained? "So I will be looking sharp."

"You're damn right. Sharp as cheddar."

"So you're directing the fleets of Interlochen folks from the Hausers?"

"Yeah . . ." Grey's thoughts trailed off and his voice grew faint. "How is she?"

"You know . . ."

"Right."

I ran upstairs, the giant eulogy in my hands, and threw my closet open. Sitting on the edge of my bed, it suddenly hit me that every single detail about this day was going to linger in my memory for the rest of my life. No pressure.

What lay ahead of me: A temple I'd never even seen before. A ceremony I'd never witnessed. Relatives I didn't know. Relatives I didn't like. Relatives that definitely don't like me. Strangers. Fourteen pages of amnesia-eulogy, plus frizzy monster hair and a face crusted with drool.

Whatever you do, I thought, *don't wear the wrong outfit.*

Meanwhile, in another part of the house, Lilly appeared in the doorway of the downstairs spare bedroom. Half dressed and clutching Oboe, she approached Kent.

"Her grandmother just called. I think she wants to have a second funeral reception."

Kent stared at her.

"I'm just bringing you the news."

"What?" Kent bit the word—this was not the time.

"Well, I mean, what's the difference between one funeral reception and two funeral receptions?" Lilly replied, trying to be conciliatory.

"What's the diff—! It's 100 percent more Silber funeral reception!"

"So . . . no?"

"Why are you asking me?"

"I can't do this. I have to play a complicated a cappella oboe solo in my best friend's father's funeral in a mystery temple for a crowd of hundreds in about three hours."

"I am reading poems!" he wailed.

"Oh please, you are reading *two* poems! Furthermore, Kent, I am asking you this because I think you and I have somehow ended up in charge!" Lilly's eyes widened—blazing and lined with moisture. They stood there on either side of the doorway and stared at one another in silence. Because it was true.

"Anyone can do whatever they want." barked Kent. "We are not going. We are all staying in this house unless Al and Cathy decide they want to have 8000 percent more funeral, which I highly doubt. Tune your oboe."

Somewhere inside me, I decided that I would not be wearing black to this funeral. This, in fact, is not going to be a funeral, it is going to be a celebration, and a concert and a recital and a reunion and I was going to get glam *dammit* and I dared anyone to stop me because I was feeling just feisty enough to start hurting feelings.

My hand grazes my senior MORP dress—hot pink sassiness. *Too much*, I think. I wouldn't want the good folks at the Mystery Temple to be put off. Vintage A-line Donna Reed statement? No, too "Hi Honey, I'm home and by the way, Dad is dead."

Then there it was. My hand graced the lightest green ball gown you had ever seen. It was modest and elegant, dancing on the cusp of child and fully fledged woman, and made of raw silk. *This was the one.*

Heels. The pearls my father bought me for my high school graduation just four months ago. A matching jacket in case the Mystery Temple was mysteriously cold.

I walked into the hallway and saw my mother dressed in a lavender ball gown of her own.

"It's a celebration," she said, zipping herself up.

We hadn't talked about it. It just was.

"So," I asked Lilly ten minutes later, "what do you think?"

"I think you run the risk of alienating—"

"The homecoming queen?" I interrupt.

"Your entire family."

She was right.

"Perfect," I said, and I made my way down the stairs.

The Mystery Temple was, in fact, Temple Beth Israel of Bloomfield Hills, Michigan, located on Telegraph Road, approximately five miles away.

There was a large caravan of Interlochen kids all arriving in various cars from the Hausers' house. Midwestern minivans began to fill the parking lot on the Indian summer morning, and someone drove my mom's Jeep back and forth, packing the car full of teenagers in shifts. People walked at slow paces, people arrived in suits, with fallen faces, and a sea of artistic teenagers all dressed in sobering colors, none of whom knew what to say or do besides hold one another and stay uncharacteristically quiet.

I don't remember how I got there, but, once I did, I walked through the main entrance doorway. As I went through the open temple doors, I noticed that the guest book outside was already three-quarters of the way full of signatures and messages.

I couldn't look.

I had a job to do.

I caught sight of Rabbi Syme, who was standing at the entrance to his private office. He was waiting for me.

"Ready?" he said.

"Yes," I replied, certain.

Rabbi Syme's eyes smiled at me and he nodded. Then, gesturing to me to follow, he led me inside the chamber.

"I will make certain I mention all of the details before I introduce you," he said. "I will mention the facts. You talk about your father." He stopped, then turned, and looking into me said, "Just like you did the other day."

I nodded, grateful.

Inside the temple, the ceremony began. Mom and I were on the left side, below the podium; my father's family was on the right. The aisle separated us like the parting of the Red Sea.

I clutched my speech as Michael Arden sang in his finest suit, fighting emotion during a song about a man on a baseball field that he had his friend at Juilliard copy down from a recording. Uncle Eli played his guitar. Lilly was up next and played with her eyes locked straight ahead of her, playing it with that signature singing voice that rose in a mournful cry out over the full-to-bursting congregation. The notes wailed long after the piece had ceased and no one could applaud.

And Kent, of all people, wept as he recited Carl Sandburg—his face filling and turning to the right before collecting himself and finishing, "and my prayers for you, my deep and silent prayers."

There were prayers. The cantor sang. And then Rabbi Syme took to the podium and did what he had promised. He greeted us and spoke of death. He quoted scripture and the Torah. He mentioned my father's date and place of birth, and the names of every member of his family.

And then he left it to me.

As I stood and made my way up the steps, I did not look at my mother or squeeze Kent's hand. This was a journey to the stage unlike any other I had, or would, ever take and I was ready. I placed my speech on top of the lectern and took a breath. I looked out over the congregation—the full and pulsing ocean of faces, those filling every pew and those spilling over the sides and standing in the back, huddled together like anxious, injured sailors at the demise of a captain.

I looked down at the words I had written and could not bring myself to begin.

At last I felt a hand upon my shoulder, and a murmur in my ear.

"Here," whispered Rabbi Syme, gently lifting my speech and placing the Torah beneath it, "Holy words for your own to stand upon." He squeezed my shoulder harder. "It will give you strength."

And I began.

You don't need to read everything I said that day; in many ways, you know already what I would have said, but the ending I will share. It was from C. S. Lewis's final book appropriately entitled *The Last Battle* from the Narnia Chronicles. My father had read every single installment to me as a young girl, with the exception of *The Last Battle* because we loved the stories so much that we didn't want them to be over. Well, now it was my turn to finish it for both of us:

> The term is over: the holidays have begun. The dream is ended: this is the morning.
>
> And as Aslan spoke He no longer looked to them like a lion; but the things that began to happen after that were so great and beautiful that I cannot write them.
>
> And for us this is the end of all the stories, and we can most truly say that they all lived happily ever after. But for them it was only the beginning of the real story. All their life in this world, and

all their adventures in Narnia had only been the cover and the title page: now at last they were beginning Chapter One of the Great Story, which no one on earth has read: which goes on forever: in which every chapter is better than the one before.

And then it was over and the After began.

No one tells you to be prepared to greet and console every person your father ever knew immediately following a funeral service. The moment the funeral ended, all I recall is standing up and being greeted with an inundation of faces.

Lilly and Kent touched my hands and nodded as they ran outside to the cars to make it back to our house to prepare 1367 for a stampede of visitors. Grey could not join them; he was a mess, the most earnest, sincere, well-dressed mess I have ever seen him in before or since. With a friend keeping him upward and mobile, he shuffled toward me and could not hide his swollen face. He hugged me. "I love you," he said, still crying, and moved on.

The Interlochen gang approached in droves, one by one, in clumps, they surrounded me and cheered me on. "What a speech," the faceless people uttered, holding and supporting me. "What a thing you've done." The crowd made their way through and out toward the parking lot.

Teachers. Family friends. Neighbors.

My childhood best friend Arielle approached. We had been going through a rough patch—the kind growing girls go through and some-times outgrow and sometimes don't, though I think I always knew Arielle and I would eventually find our way back to sisterhood. I almost couldn't believe she had made the trip up from Ann Arbor for the service, but, as she approached me, all I did was hold her hands as she broke down in sobs. Arielle, distraught, showed her love for me, for my dad, and for life itself.

Strangers. Distant cousins. Business associates.

David and Robin approached, in their best clothes and smiling sadly. "Your dad would be so proud of what you just did," said David, in a fragmented voice. They both hugged me and as they left I knew they would look after me forever.

Teenagers. Children. Men and women from every walk of life.

And then that was over and I looked over to see my father's family swiftly exiting the building in great distress. *Oh my God.* In my eulogy, I had been careful to avoid committing the ultimate crime. With a stage all to myself, I could have used that platform to air every grievance, every malignant word, every oppressive act.

But I didn't do that. I did something worse.

I didn't mention them at all.

Reception! Yet Another Farce

(*At rise: A medium-sized 1960s colonial house on a quiet street in a sleepy suburb—the house could be any house, the street any street, the suburb any suburb, anywhere. But this particular house is located in front of a river, the River Rouge to be exact, in Birmingham, Michigan, beside the large fairway of a community golf course. Fairway is, in fact, the name of the street we see as the afternoon light begins to expose the scene like a vintage Polaroid. The house is the third on the right, between 1373 (the Home of the Gay Couple with the lively boxer) and 1345 (the Family of Four with the two genius boys). This is 1367— home of THE SILBER FAMILY, with a garden in front, a wisteria tree, and a white fence. Just like in all of the movies. But this is not a movie. This is real life. Though it may not feel that way today.*)

(*Enter KENT, breathless, from outside.*)

KENT: Where should everyone park?
AL: I don't know.
KENT: (*on a cell phone to Lilly, who is herself directing someone on their way to 1367*) Are people allowed to park in the street?
AL: I don't know.
KENT: (*to Lilly*) She doesn't know.

AL: My neighbors are all coming over, so I'm sure they wouldn't mind people parking in their driveways if you ask.

KENT: *(He looks out the window, considers.)* OK. I'm on it. *(He exits. A pause. He reenters.)* Poo, how do I know who is a neighbor versus who is the Evil Brigade?

AL: You'll know.

KENT: OK, I'm on it.

(KENT exits.)

(To further the earlier description of the house, 1367 is located on the Rouge Riverbank, along a steep hill that empties into the river itself, a river that threatened several times, and once did indeed flood the lower level of the house entirely, causing CATHERINE to rip up the carpeting and tile the entire downstairs level in a pastel peach granite. Herself. With spackle. That was in 1996. In the autumn and winter months, the tile is very cold beneath one's feet. As it is October the tile is, predictably, terribly cold today.)

(GREY enters, his face is swollen and red, his voice is drenched in tears and self-deprecating sarcasm.)

GREY: I'm here.

(He is embarrassed, but not embarrassed, at his open weeping. His suit is only slightly disheveled. All of this, in this circumstance, is both elegant and hilarious.)

GREY: What do you need me to do?

AL: Set up some chairs?

GREY: *(Blows his nose.)* Who is doing the food?

AL: You are.

GREY: Oh Christ. I'll get on that as soon as I finish sniveling grotesquely.

(*Because of the house's location along a steep hill, 1367 technically has three levels—the "top floor," where the private rooms are located; the "upstairs," which is technically the middle level that contains the kitchen, main living and dining rooms; and the "downstairs" bottom level located below the waterline of the river. This you can see from the more casual sofas in what is known as "the other living room," which sits beside the guest bedroom with an accompanying half-bath and leads out to the garage. So you see, much of the house is made of only half-levels, with many tiny steps and slants to accommodate the slope of the hill, which cuts through the house diagonally.*)

Like this:

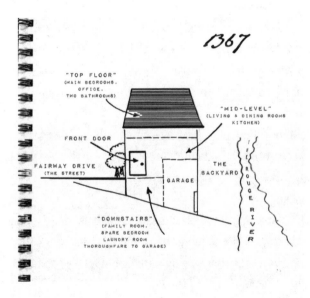

GREY: OK, I'm just going to put everything in your refrigerator onto your dining room table in so spectacular a design that no one will notice how awful all the donation food is or that Kent and I ate our feelings—AKA all the dessert—last night, while we were ironing everything.

AL: Great.

(From this position, you will also note that the top floor is the location of all the bedrooms—the master bedroom as well as AL's, an office, and a half bath at the top of the stairs. The stairwell walls are practically wall-papered with family photographs from every era and generation.)

(LILLY enters from the front door.)

LILLY: Everyone is coming and there is no parking.

AL: I thought we could park on the street.

LILLY: The street is full.

AL: What about our neighbors' driveways?

LILLY: The neighbors' driveways are full.

AL: How many people can there be?

LILLY: There were approximately six million people at the funeral. *(off AL's blank expression)* Give or take.

AL: Well people will have to walk, I guess.

LILLY: Four of the six million attendees were senior citizens.

AL: Evil ones!

LILLY: Right, but think of it this way– we can't have one of them die on the way to your dad's funeral reception, because it would take the focus away from your dad's funeral.

AL: That's fair.

LILLY: I also don't want the police to get suspicious that they had to show up to your house more than once this week.

AL: *(considering)* Put someone on parking duty. Like valet. Like the two little boys in *Father of the Bride*.

LILLY: Oh, I love that part!

AL: Me too!

(LILLY exits, dialing her cell phone.)

(From the doorway, you can also see that the downstairs "other living room" has two long sofas around a small glass coffee table, dotted with extra chairs, all prepared to be sat upon.)

(*CATHERINE enters from the top floor, having changed out of her lavender ball gown and into a simple black dress. She has freshened up her face, pulled back her hair, and is now a vision of quiet resignation and fortitude.*)

CATHERINE: They're coming.

(*Then a long moment without words. There is a hum of distant cars, soft voices, then the ringing of the doorbell. AL opens the front door. ALL enter. Bedlam. Everyone is talking at once.*)

MRS. SOMETHING-BAUM: And so I said to Edna, "It's shameful, just shameful how that little *shiksa* didn't even mention them and she left it completely to the rabbi."

MRS. WHOEVER-WITZ: I *know.*

MRS. SOMETHING-BAUM: I mean who raised a child like that? (*spotting CATHERINE*) Oh, there she is. (*hugging*) Oh Cathy, so sorry for your loss.

MR. NOSEY-BACH: Is there a deli platter?

MRS. NOSEY-BACH: (*hard of hearing*) Eh?

MR. NOSEY-BACH: IS THERE FOOD?

MRS. NOSEY-BACH: *EH?!*

(*It is becoming evident that all of ALBERT and EDNA SILBER's elderly friends are settling into the upstairs living room, taking over and seemingly multiplying in the scattered chairs like brooms in* The Sorcerer's Apprentice—*while all of the young artsy teenagers are migrating to the downstairs living room. Entirely separate and sealed worlds.*)

(*Enter AARON, a delightfully neurotic Woody Allen-esque intellectual with a heart of gold.*)

AARON: Al? Hi. We're having a little trouble with the people

downstairs. The folks don't have food. And they're, well, you know,
understandably, afraid of going upstairs to the food table.

AL: (*trying to make out his meaning*) Are you saying you want me
to bring down a platter of meat and cheese and crudités or are you
saying you want me to ask the Pharaoh to "let my people go?"

AARON: (*pause*). Yes.

AL: OK. (*she calls upstairs*) Grey!

GREY: Yeah?

AL: Provisions.

GREY: On it.

(*GREY returns at lightning speed carrying trays of food in his giant arms.*)

AL: Are Rebel Forces gathering?

GREY: Flying monkeys are circling Mount Doom.

(*AARON, GREY, and AL descend the stairs and place the trays on the
coffee table below. Lights up on the separate scenes on the sofas up and
downstairs.*)

JESSICA: Part of me thinks this is really nice.

MICHAEL ARDEN: What do you mean?

JESSICA: You know, all of us, scattered all over the world, so far away
from everyone we love so much in such a unique, Interlochen way,
all longing to be back together? And here we are.

MICHAEL ARDEN: All back together?

JESSICA: Yeah.

BIG-HAIRED LADY: (*with shoulders padded like a lunatic's cell*)
Cathy, I never really "got" Michael, but I'm sorry he's gone.

CATHERINE: Thank you?

(*At long last, the SILBERS arrive. Brother, sister, sister's life partner, and
trailing at the end, ALBERT and EDNA.*)

LIFE-PARTNER: (*looking at the photos on the wall, scowling*) Just *look* at this. There is not a *single* picture of them. No wonder they feel abandoned!

AUNT: It's shameful.

LIFE-PARTNER: It makes me sick.

(*KENT and GREY look on around the corner, whispering.*)

GREY: Do we tell them to turn around and look at all the pictures of the Silbers right behind her?

KENT: Nah.

GREY: Why not?

KENT: I don't know, the lesbian life-partner looks like a little bit of a loose canon, and I like to keep my distance from people who might stab me.

MRS. SOMETHING-BAUM: Edna, what a tragedy. That girl's eulogy was an outrage . . .

MRS. WHOEVER-WITZ: How old is Cathy? Fifty-two? Eh. That's young. She'll find someone else . . .

(*The YOUNG PEOPLE, and everyone associated with AL and CATHERINE are now communing downstairs in the other living room, telling stories, trying to laugh, and holding one another in what appears to everyone upstairs to be an almost sickening display of overt affection. It is in this moment that KENT realizes that there is one who is not among them. LILLY is missing, and has been missing for quite some time. He grabs JESSICA.*)

KENT: Jess! Where did Lilly go?

JESSICA: (*turning*) I . . . she's . . . doing something.

KENT: Like what?

JESSICA: I don't know.

KENT: OK, well, would you pull her out of whatever it is she's doing?

JESSICA: (*Vietnam War movie voice*) Kent— she's *stuck*. With the Silbers. Upstairs.

KENT: (*checking upstairs, drill sergeant voice!!*) Well, put on a helmet and pads and get in there!

(*LILLY, is indeed upstairs, and she is tending to ALBERT personally, her hazel eyes wide and patient, as ALBERT sits in the center of the room with his address book open on his lap and a large, black Sharpie in his hand, which he is using to mark people out of the address book as God might mark them off the face of the earth entirely. LILLY looks on just as he swipes black across "1367 Fairway . . .")*

LILLY: Albert, is there anything I can get you?

ALBERT: (*not looking up*) A turkey sandwich.

LILLY: Coming up.

ALBERT: (*calling after her*) On rye.

LILLY: (*smiling, drowning him in her sweetness*) No problem.

(*LILLY exits to make the perfect turkey sandwich. Suddenly AL confronts her at the food table in the dining room, having snuck over through the kitchen.*)

AL: What are you doing?

LILLY: Shhhhh!

AL: (*whispering*) What are you doing?

LILLY: I am tending to your grandparents.

AL: Who are you, Benedict Arnold?

LILLY: Al.

AL: *Et tu, Brute?*

LILLY: Al! I'm tending to your horrible grandparents so you don't have to!

AL: Why?

LILLY: Shh! (*She looks over her shoulder at ALBERT and his Address Book of Doom.*) Because someone has to. Someone has to make them think this is about them—all about them, not just a little bit, all.

AL: Why didn't you tell me this was your plan?

LILLY: (*eyebrow cocked*) I thought you might overreact—

AL: Ah. Noted.

LILLY: —and that is what best friends are for, so now I am making Albert a turkey sandwich. On rye.

AL: Lilly, I love you.

LILLY: I love you too. (*cutting the corners off of the bread.*) And I intend to get through this afternoon by catching these nasty, *nasty* flies with honey.

(*She exits, sandwich in hand.*)

LILLY: Here you go, Albert. Turkey on rye.

ALBERT: Did you use mustard?

LILLY: (*Miss America smile cracking at the corners*) . . . No.

ALBERT: I wanted mustard.

LILLY: (*brittle.*) Coming right up.

(*Hours pass just as that one did. People come and go, ALBERT and EDNA's friends ignore AL and CATHERINE, and the other way around. Tension. Turkey sandwiches. People shoving more bagels onto the dining room table and matzo ball soup into the freezer. Many people are going to compare this funeral to the ones in* The Big Chill *or* Passed Away *or* Steel Magnolias. *They'll say, "Those were great films." But this funeral is not like those funerals at all. This funeral totally sucks.*)

(*AL rubs at her temples and makes her way over to GREY, who is nursing a drink.*)

AL: What is the status of upstairs?

GREY: A Whoever-Blat or a Whatever-Stein just offered your grandmother a sedative called Nembutal.

AL: Yeah.

GREY: Well, it inspired me to pour myself a sedative called Bombay Sapphire . . .

(*LILLY enters from upstairs, flushed. Nervous.*)

LILLY: Al? Edna wants to talk to you.

AL: (*taken aback.*) What?

LILLY: I guess she is already in your bedroom, waiting. On the top floor.

(*AL nods to LILLY and makes her way to the top of the stairs. This will not be the last conversation someone from the SILBERS wants to have with her before the end of the day. There will be yelling from her AUNT and the LESBIAN LIFE-PARTNER in the hall. There will be an awkward walk down the street with the long-lost family members. There will be dead silence from ALBERT. But before continuing to the top floor, AL takes LILLY's hand and looks down at CATHERINE, her mother's friends, and above all, at the horde, the throng, the sheer enormous motley battalion of loving friends she has been blessed to have. Standing at the top of the staircase, all AL can do is laugh at all that has transpired.*)

The Protagonist Attempts Existential Escape

(A Diagram)

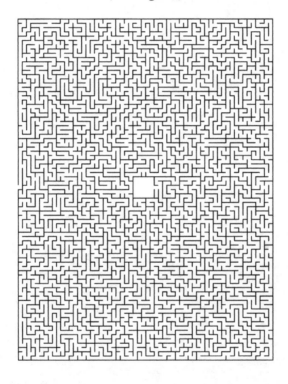

Edna

S he took me upstairs to talk.

I now realize Edna likely wanted to express her hurt. I hadn't mentioned anyone from my father's side of the family in the eulogy. Of course that would be hurtful.

But Edna was a good woman, wasn't she? So often it was hard to tell.

Her days seemed consumed by envy of the well-lived lives of others. With such vile bigotry, she had condemned my mother's character and non-Jewishness, she diminished my mother for possessing flourishing artistic gifts. When her daughter Deborah became an undisputed expert in her quilting field, Edna started her own quilt collection—commandeering and attempting to outshine Deborah.

Once, early in their marriage, a sophisticated expatriate neighbor of Edna's named Elsie Greenberg bonded with my mother on her first visit to the Silber's condo in Sarasota. Elsie was vibrant, cultured and worldly, and responded to my mother Catherine's artistic sensibilities with great enthusiasm, and vice versa. Elsie invited the Silber family to dessert after the traditional Passover seder later that week, and excited, my mother accepted and reported the invitation to Edna a few hours later. She was met with Edna's silence as she slowly stirred a pot of soup at the stove. "Oh," Edna said quietly as she continued to stir, "you haven't heard. Elsie passed away this afternoon. Quite suddenly. I am so sorry, Catherine."

Days later, in the condo's elevator, my devastated mother was shocked to see, of all people, Elsie Greenberg: *not dead,* and sorry to have missed them. When my mother explained that they didn't come over for dessert because Edna had falsely reported their potential host as *deceased*, Elsie shook her head and sighed, "That is just so *Edna.*"

But this was also the woman who flew out to San Francisco (despite grave warnings from her overbearing husband) to talk to Deborah face-to-face after she had come out in a vitriolic letter to her parents.

This was the woman who had heard I loved an authentic 1930s cock-tail dress at a vintage store and went right out and bought it for me.

This was the woman who wanted me to discover something that I liked enough that she could actively look for things to help me build a collection. I felt then that she forced this collection business on me—I just wasn't into nutcrackers, spiders, or lobsters nearly enough to satisfy her—but, in hindsight, I think it was her way of "grand-parenting;" of keeping me in her mind, of her fragmented form of connecting. (How I sort of wish I could tell her now that it was owls.)

I saw the repressed artistic soul—the piano teacher with a flair for jewelry, a gifted and inspired sculptor—unable to fulfill her longings, possibly jealous that I was given every freedom to do so.

This was the woman who had tried so hard to teach me to play the piano. I still have the books from the 1940s that she used to teach all those children on the block in Detroit. (I wish I had been less intimidated by both her and her piano.)

This was the woman who tried to reach out by taking me to the Fisher Theatre in downtown Detroit to see the tour of *Jekyll and Hyde* when I was fourteen. We had a wonderful day, a matinee and dinner after the show. I see now that she wanted to connect with me on a level that she knew I would appreciate. No more forced collections or wading through false histories, just the two of us in a theater. It felt like home. That was probably the best day I ever had with her.

When I was a child—probably about five years old—I drew a portrait of her—a crude pen-and-marker drawing. I gave it to her hoping she would like it. But she looked down and saw the way a child had drawn her age—wrinkles and all—and was hurt. I hadn't intended to break her heart in any way. Still, she took me aside and told me, "One day you will have wrinkles and be old too, and there is nothing wrong with that." I wanted to tell her that I knew that. I was just trying to draw a picture of my grandma—that was all.

She was the woman who taught me how to play a form of solitaire called "Thirteen." She would patiently watch me assemble and disassemble the cards over and over again. It wasn't until today, as I am sitting here writing this, that I realized my grandmother was a highly sensitive woman with an artistic temperament. A faded beauty who, like so many from her generation, was handed from her father to her husband before she had any emotional skills, actualized dreams, or even a concept of self. She was taken from one shelf and placed upon another, made to conform by bearing children, and be grateful for things she never asked for. Her whole life was a form of solitaire.

All these truths aside, I would never be able to forget how profoundly she screamed at Rabbi Syme that Tuesday, even as her son's body lay upstairs. How hatefully she screamed the word *shiksa* and protested that I "didn't even know him."

It wasn't that I didn't know him. It was that they didn't know me.

"Alex," I braced myself for a God-knows-what, "you understand that you are a disgrace to us? I don't even know where to begin to—"

She went on like that for a while. My mind filled with white noise as I watched her cataloguing my lifelong list of offenses in silent slow motion, the female, Jewish Grand Inquisitor in the trial of my teenaged character. *Will they or won't they burn me at the stake?* I thought. *Well, it is Friday, they'd better decide pretty soon or they'll have to wait and burn me after Shabbat.*

I watched her pained expression, I wanted to tell her that I understood— that it was OK that she didn't know or like me. It was alright that this was true because first, I didn't think much of dishonesty and this family was rife with it; and second, and more crucially, I understood that I wasn't very likeable. At least not to her.

"You know what, Grandma?" I interrupted her heresy monologue, "You've made your point. Let's just say it. Let's get it out in the open— none of you have ever really liked me."

She gasped, thunderstruck. She covered her face, eyes transfixed with horror—like a vampire stopped in its tracks by the garlic covered cross of my blatant honesty. That was when I saw it: her hands.

Back when my extended family was still speaking to me, people were always coming up to me and remarking upon how greatly I resembled Edna. I suppose I'm aware now that that is no small compliment. I don't see it. Perhaps because I don't want to, perhaps because I can't see beauty in myself, or perhaps because I never really knew her so I cannot see her face in mine.

But we have the same hands.

There they were, covering her horror-struck face, completely in awe of the fact that her granddaughter had just taken it there.

You know what's awesome? Irony. People my age learned what it means from Alanis Morissette, so our grasp is tenuous at best, but when it plays out over life and death situations it can get pretty trippy.

Small, with large palms and fingers prone to swelling, nail beds like a child's, dry cuticles, skin baby soft, and subtly expressive. They look as if they were created to work hard, to milk cows, to cook, freeze, and scrub. They are not long and lean; they are not what you see in magazines. They are the hands of a feminine warrior—the kind of hands jewelry looks out of place on, rings laugh, bracelets scoff, the hands are too humble, too common looking to support the grandiosity of adornment. When I look down at my hands, it is undeniable—I see her clumsily cutting onions; I see her coaxing immaculate, expressive birds out of marble; I see her wrinkles and age and know that "there is nothing wrong with that."

Oh, Edna, I did not know you, and there are terrorist cells more nurturing than you.

But I have your hands.

And that is the possibility of something.

Funeral-ku Two

4.
Once the party's done
only a tank remains. Of
unused oxygen.

An Afterplay

(*The theater is dark. The play has been over for hours and yet AL sits alone in the middle of the hushed auditorium, thick with darkness. One can only make the proscenium out by the faintest lights from the street that cascade through and across the back walls. AL cannot move, the darkness within her as thorough as the darkness without, and she stares into the spaces where, only moments ago the seats were full; charged with laughter and compassion, with sorrow and song, with overflowing energy and rapt attention. Everyone has gone—on their trains, their buses, in their cars and away onto planes, and she thinks:* there is nothing, no feeling in the world like sitting in an empty theater after a performance. *It is almost as if you can convince yourself that it happened. You recall that just a moment ago there was a glint of magic in the air of this very room, and it was so recent a breath ago you can still feel the crackle of it in the air.*

But now it is gone. Just like that.

Suddenly a door unhinges. If AL had the wherewithal to turn, she would, but before long she can smell who it is—that cologne, so specific and familiar. It is MIKE, *the* STAGE MANAGER, *and he sits beside AL, settling there without a word. She sits that way for a long while before Mike speaks.*)

MIKE: Good show tonight. *(He speaks below his breath, his voice slicing into the darkness.)*

AL: Yes.

(MIKE sits up, and leans forward, running his hands over the wood and brass and velvet of the seats before settling his arms over the seatback and releasing a deep sigh. It's the kind of sigh from a man who has not taken a good breath in a long while.)

MIKE: You know this is my last show?

AL: Yes.

(AL keeps her eyes soft-focused on the emptiness before her, for if she does not, if she looks at him, or anywhere but straight ahead she will not be able to go on. MIKE nods and digs into his pocket. Then, reaching gently for her hand, he lifts and opens it, and deposits a ring of heavy keys inside.)

MIKE: To the theater.

AL: But what about the leading lady?

MIKE: Oh, she's here.

AL: But I don't know how to look after a theater.

MIKE: You will have to learn.

AL: All by myself?

MIKE: You'll learn.

(MIKE touches her shoulder as he stands up, looking around. The light from the streets is beginning to flood the theater more intensely now, so that you can see his face illuminated as he inhales the scent of it all— the musk of everything—from the must and damp, to the sweat, and to the sheer electricity in the air before making his way up the center aisle, jumping onto the stage itself, and, looking to AL, taking a long bow before turning on his heel and walking off the stage toward the light pouring in from the world beyond. She is holding the keys to a darkened theater. And the leading lady cannot go on.)

PART THREE:
THE AFTERMATH

Memories through Lenses

In the spring of 2013, I made my Carnegie Hall debut in a very strange little operetta called *Song of Norway*. Ted Sperling conducted the Collegiate Chorale and the American Symphony Orchestra. The show was narrated by Jim Dale and the cast included Santino Fontana (a great old friend from Interlochen in 1999, as well as my brief tenure at University of Minnesota), Jason Danieley, and two-time Tony Award-winner Judy Kaye.

The score is a beast, and, while it's not exactly Wagner, everyone was singing at the very top of their game, like athletes preparing for the 2013 singing Olympics. The fourth-rate book was a specious biographical account of composer Edvard Grieg (Santino), his wife (me), his best friend (Jason), and an opera diva (Judy). It was set in Norway, and there was a perplexing plotline that contained magical trolls and the making of invisible cakes for the midsummer festival. I didn't exactly follow this so-called "plot," and I was *in* the damn thing, but suffice it to say, we all sounded terrific and Jim Dale filled all the plot holes with a heck of a lot of charm.

I was very nervous, not only because it was a "big sing" but also because I was the least famous person in the cast and, above all, because I harbored a memory of Judy Kaye that was so important to me, I didn't even begin to know how to behave in front of her.

You know that feeling? When an artist's music, writing, teachings, leadership, or public advocacy is so vital to your individual narrative that you feel as though you not only owe them an open letter and a thank you fruit basket, but in a strange way you feel as though you actually know them, when in fact you do not. They have palpably touched your life.

One night, Jason, Judy and I were out promoting the concert performance at the Pierre (a fancy hotel in midtown Manhattan), performing for Queen Sonja of Norway (I know, I know, but this is real) and a room full of cultural attachés and Norwegian celebrants. Dressed in our finest and sitting in the kitchen (a scenario every actor is familiar with), the three of us prepared to sing for the Queen. Of Norway.

I looked over at Judy and noticed her face betraying sadness; surrounded by the din of the kitchen, she rubbed her hands and stared off into the distance. The aura that was always around her now appeared to tremble, and I made my way over and asked what was on her mind.

She smiled faintly. "My father recently died," she replied. "I just . . . miss him."

My heart lurched. I had come to know this ache so well.

In spending the last decade and change mitigating my own feelings on grief, I had come to learn so much about the greatest democracy in all of humanity: the Democracy of Loss. Despite time period, language, culture, age, social mores, or faith, the fear of losing someone you love has kept human beings up at night since we were cognizant enough to have thoughts.

Grief is not a contest, and pain is relative. There is not a "better" kind of loss or a "better" time in someone's life to lose a beloved—loss is loss—at any stage of one's life, the loss is monumental, the pain indefatigable, and each stage comes with its own set of complexities. But what I know for certain is that we are all children, really, when our parents die, and sometimes the more difficult the relationship, the more exquisite the pain of their absence.

All of this to say: that night, as I gazed upon two-time Tony-winner Judy Kaye—dressed in black tie and sitting in a kitchen about to sing for the Queen of Norway—I knew that despite her adulthood, her every success, her pain was one I knew.

Profoundly.

"I understand," I said.

In the faux silence of clanking dishes and Jason Danieley warming up gloriously in the background, I took her hand. I knew *this* was the moment to tell her.

"You know," I began, "one of the hardest things I learned when my own my father died, was the realization that every single person I ever met from that moment on, was never going to meet or know him. I found that so difficult."

"Indeed," she nodded.

"But it is magical little moments like this one, that prove that almost anything is possible. Because Judy? You have met my dad. You have met my mom, too, and me. We all met you in the lobby of *Ragtime* in 1998. It was during the winter BC/EFA collection and we bought a poster from you with a one-hundred-dollar bill, and you spoke to all of us."

Judy turned to me and stared. Her face went white. As a surge of memory flooded her, tears surfaced. She blinked.

"I remember." She gasped. "I remember you."

❛ ❜

In 1998, the actors had gathered in the aisles and the lobby of Ford Center for the Performing Arts on Forty-second Street for the semiannual Broadway Cares/Equity Fights AIDS collection, and, as they did, my family approached Alex Strange (the original Little Boy), Stephen Sutcliffe (the original Mother's Younger Brother) and most thrilling of all, the actress who originated the role of Emma Goldman: Tony winner Judy Kaye.

My entire family was a puddle. We were in emotional pieces as we approached the trio; all holding red buckets and, what I found so remarkable (at fourteen and so Broadway-bitten) was that they were so normal! They were not gods or sorcerers, but real, breathing people. Real people in costume at the end of their "shift," raising money coin by coin for AIDS. My mother proudly handed Judy Kaye a hundred-dollar bill; she gave it to her with both hands, like the exchange was a holy thing—which it was—as she purchased a poster signed by the entire company. (One that, to this day, hangs upon my wall.)

I was speechless. So shy, and so emotionally decimated by *Ragtime* and by my first live Broadway experience that both Mom and I let Dad do the talking, for he was best at it. Dad had a way of humanizing everyone he met—making each person who crossed his path feel seen, respected, and understood, while also reminding everyone that we were all part of the human race. To this day, I never knew how he achieved that every single time he opened his mouth.

Without warning Dad began to talk about me.

Oh God, I thought. *Oh no—don't tell them about me*! When you are fourteen, almost every single thing that happens to a person is beyond embarrassing, and, at the time, I thought I would shrivel up and die from the embarrassment of my dad telling this trio of Broadway actors that I had been in *all* the school plays, and that one day it was my dream (and his) that I would be up there telling important Broadway stories, just like them.

There was a pause. *Oh God, oh God*, I thought. I assumed these actors were internally rolling their eyes, dismissing us utterly, having heard that speech from countless goober parents every day. In that pause I hoped the theater would open beneath my feet and swallow me whole (like Gandalf and the evil Balrog creature) to avoid having to endure a single millisecond more of the agony of my father's belief and pride in all that I was becoming.

But dismissal is not what happened.

Judy Kaye turned from my dad and gazed at me, her look trenchant, thoughtful, as if she were surveying my destiny. After a moment of appraisal she replied, "You will."

Have you ever found yourself *inside* a moment that you know will define you? This was one of mine. When I die, in my autopsy, the medical examiner will remove my organs and see, sketched upon my heart, a fully documented account of that moment, for it is tattooed there. Every scrap of that memory shall be holy to me for all eternity.

The Silbers left the theater that night and went into the streets of New York City, taking with them a poster and a memory that none of them would ever forget.

I finished recounting the story to Judy as kitchen staff darted and swarmed and the event director informed us we had five minutes until show time.

"I remember. I told you that you would, and you have," Judy said, quite dazed with it all. "I remember. Your family was special; there was something about you. I guess you really never know who you are affecting —what ripples are caused by the slightest of things." She thought for a moment, "And I remember him. Your dad. I remember. How remarkable to meet you like this in the present."

Your greatness is not what you have. It's what you give.

The Laugh

The Funeral Reception of Doom did, eventually, end.

As "the upstairs people" retreated, we closed the door on the last of their troops and began to take the upstairs—and subsequently the entire house—back. Those who remained spread their wings and (literally) danced in the yard. They dared to eat directly from the food table (and the fridge and the gift baskets). We sang show tunes while Aaron played around on my mother's vintage Chickering piano. One might almost have thought we were—God forbid—celebrating.

After an hour or so, the people who were still students at Interlochen had to return to campus and, as our own numbers dwindled, the remainder of our group (which included my mother's friends, as well as a handful of mine who had gotten the entire weekend off from college). We piled provisions into the car, and headed over to the Steinmans' house for what could only be described as an epic dessert *wake*. It was time to cut loose at our very own second funeral reception, which eliminated the crazy people and included everyone's very favorite thing: dessert.[16]

Fran Steinman had a glorious kitchen, the kind you picture all of the cooks on the Food Network having in their homes: two sinks, each with power hoses, state-of-the-art ovens, a giant Midwestern-sized refrigerator,

---

16   Fran Steinman makes some serious (and non-yellow) dessert. Do not get between that woman and a power mixer.

plus immaculately arranged cupboards, majestic marble countertops, and pantries that exist only in the imaginations of the world's greatest food artists.

Fran expresses herself in food, and her outpouring of love for my father Michael and all things Silber was overwhelming. There were brownies and four different kind of cookies, hand-whipped cream, coffees, chocolates, and her prize-winning cheesecakes. But the pièce de résistance was a cherries jubilee. That's right: flambé. Fran had prepared it expressly, as flambé had featured in the production of *She Loves Me* the Interlochen theater majors had all done nearly a year earlier. Now, as we all gathered in the kitchen around the flambé, everyone began to clap for the flaming dessert. We cheered, took plates, filled them to the brim with Fran's confections, and retired to the cozy living room for an inordinate amount of sugar-fueled merriment.

That evening at the Steinmans' was the reception I will always choose to remember, when everyone relaxed and smiled and celebrated not only Michael Silber's life, but life itself. It was friends gathered together from every corner of the country, eating delicious food, telling stories, recalling memories, and performing parlor tricks as only theater people can. If you had looked into the window of the Steinmans' house that evening, you never would have guessed it was a funeral. It was exactly the kind of party Dad would have hosted.

But that had to end too. After we helped Fran clean up and pack away the treats, everyone had to head back to their hotels, schools, or lives, and only a remaining few of us ambled back to 1367; full, and numb and literally everything in between.

The remaining group gathered in the very seats the enemy forces had occupied hours earlier. After a while, we decided we needed real food. Mom made guacamole. Utilizing thirty or so avocados, she whipped up her killer recipe and put it in a giant salad bowl accompanied by two bags of donation tortilla chips someone had given us on the hand-painted Haitian coffee table my parents acquired in Port-au-Prince in the late 1970s.

Besides Grey, Lilly, and Kent, only Jessica and Jeremey were to remain at 1367 for the night. Jeremey was oddly occupying the place with a sense of real ownership. At the time, he did know the place far better than anyone, after all. He belonged there.

Jessica did too; she was mayor of our inner circle and my other dearest friend. The previous summer, we'd roomed together while working at camp and had driven to lakes for midnight swims, to the E-Z Mart for emergency popsicles, and to Honor, Michigan, to stare at the stars on the hood of her vintage pickup truck.

We decided to take a walk on the unseasonably warm October evening. It smelled of first fires and Michigan musk, the kind of evening that makes you think you are within the pages of a nostalgic novel. The sky was like a painting—deepest purple at the edges with a brick-colored moon, and dried leaves glittering like precious gold, amber, and ruby. In hindsight, I think Jessica was trying to give me permission to let go with her, to give me safe passage away from the public stage of grief and family and even our friends. But the truth was, even if I had wanted to let it go, I didn't know how. Saying as much, she took my hand and we walked in silence before coming upon the local high school homecoming dance, which we promptly went to—for about twenty minutes—laughing our heads off at the oddity of it all before turning back.

Last to arrive home were Grey, Kent, and Lilly. They'd dropped everyone off at their buses, airports, or various hotels.

"We come bearing more food," Grey droned. They entered holding enormous bags of food from their various drop-off points, though no bags were larger than the ones beneath their eyes. The boys withdrew to the kitchen to finish off some of the fancy 17 percent alcohol lager the German couple down the street had given us.

Lilly was silent as she entered the front doorway and soundlessly removed her clogs. She sighed as she tucked her short hair behind each ear with her precise woodwind player's fingers. She made her way up the three little steps from the entrance to the main living room. She looked exhaustedly over all of us looking exhaustedly back at her. No one spoke. It was hard to discern what Lilly was about to do.

Then, in her own bewitching way, Lilly did something that in hindsight seems so bizarre, yet so achingly inevitable, it is a wonder we ever hesitated to wonder otherwise.

She laughed.

It started modestly—a little chortle in her distinctive way, all charm and delight and Virginian sunshine fed by exhaustion, sorrow, and utter disbelief at all that had transpired. The look on her face as the laughter escaped her open mouth was brighter than any sunlight, and it flooded through the living room, drenching us with its radiance. Lilly laughed and laughed, hysterically cackling into her hands until she ugly cried.

It was a single star shining above an ocean of sadness. How could we not join her? Something had tilted. This was it—the end of the line. *You are here*, the imaginary sign proclaimed. This burnt out, fully smoked, nothing-left-but-the-filter cigarette stub of a week had come to an end.

Lilly's laughter spread and caught us all. The room erupted, everyone clutching at the arms and legs of another member of this ragtag crew, not ceasing, but growing, the sound of it mounting as tears flooded down our faces and we hit our chests in a desperate attempt to breathe.

"What's so funny?" the boys asked, entering from the kitchen.

Soon they were guffawing too. We all knew we were gathered for a sober purpose, but holy hell it felt good.

Even at the end of this horrible day, we found a way to laugh. All together. To eat guacamole. Because that is how any day should end—whether it be a funeral, a hanging, a luau, a quinceañera, or a Tuesday. And though I have never been part of a street gang, I would wager that this kind of camaraderie felt pretty close—the kind of feel good we-sure-weathered-that-storm-together type togetherness that put one in the mood to play chicken and steal a stop sign.

I never would have believed it, but as I rolled on the floor, face aching, lungs positively burning from the sheer strength and necessity of the laughter, I knew: somehow, someday, it was all going to be alright.

Someday.

The Letter from Haley

The day after the funeral, a letter arrived from Haley DeKorne.

When I had met Haley at Interlochen, we were both juniors in high school, but Haley had the special honor of being a "third-year junior," meaning she had been at Interlochen since her freshman year and would graduate as a "four-year senior"—a rare and very special designation.

Haley was a native of Traverse City, Michigan, which is not a city, really, but a large town (though it is city-like now) that is the closest city to Interlochen itself. She lived there with her mother, just the two of them. Because of her proximity, Haley was a day student and commuted in from town and only occasionally spent the night, often with Jessica, also a third-year junior.

My most significant memories of Haley were shared in what is still to this day one of the greatest acting challenges of my life, playing Annie Sullivan in *The Miracle Worker* opposite Haley as Helen Keller. It was an honor to be cast straight out of the gate at Interlochen. The talent pool was extraordinary and I was exhilarated at being able to properly cut my teeth with such talented young people—high-flying athletes who improved my own game.

I had played this role the previous year back home, and getting to revisit it was a gift. Though Annie Sullivan was a dream part, the three girls I shared the role with were the kind of mean we can only be in high school—merciless for reasons I still to this day do not understand. And as we all know, the world is mighty small at sixteen, and they likely didn't understand that my father was battling cancer and couldn't even come see me in the play. This revisitation to *The Miracle Worker* was not only a gift to my soul, for thanks to those girls I desperately needed a "do-over," but it was a chance for my father to finally see me conquer it and soar.

Robin directed Haley and I in both of our first leading roles at Interlochen. While that story of fortitude and conquering of adversity covered us in more physical bruises than we cold count, it bonded us "forever and ever"[17] and set in motion the deepest relationship to a place I still have yet to match.

After Interlochen, Haley committed to an academic track and spent the first year of college at the American University of Paris and, despite the glory of her first few weeks in Paris on her grand adventure, when everything crumbled and our mighty gang of Interlochen comrades reunited in Metro Detroit, there was a Haley-shaped hole in the scenery.

Then that Saturday, her letter arrived:

> It's 4 a.m. now, so I'm philosophizing. Thinking about distances and love. I feel all bruised inside with large pieces of my heart so physically far away. But then I think that's in my head, and that really my love is with you and my mom and everyone just as strongly now as if we were in the same room. It's just a little harder to realize it. So I hope you're able to feel your father's love, and yours for him, even if there seems to be a distance between. I think distance is like time: created for our minds, without real existence.
>
> But love does exist, really, strongly, the most absolute thing I know. So strong it causes bruises. Yes, we know all about those . . .
>
> This evening I was part of a discussion with some friends about the ever-present beggars—if one should give them money,

---

17   "forever and ever"—is a direct quote from William Gibson's *The Miracle Worker*.

if it would actually help them, etc. I think if you had been there you wouldn't have bothered with all the intellectualizing, you would have responded with that amazingly generous heart of yours (which was what the conversation needed). So I wish you had been there because it refreshes and inspires me to see that wonderful heart in action. It is truly a gift that no other talent can rival, I hope you realize that. I read a great play where one line I caught was "Vous aimez: c'est assez." Meaning: "You love: that's enough." And even though it can't always feel that simple, I'm convinced, that underneath it is.

Although because I'm human I can't help but doubt that. Each time a flower falls from my plant (her name is Lady D'Abenville) I am shaken. But in time, with patience, new buds always come. If I don't remember to look for them they can be easy to miss, but they're always there.

I'm yawning, so not having finished my work I think I'll sleep anyways. I'm proud of my priority adjustment.

I'll be with you in my sleep as I am in my days—soft breezes and lighted windows at night.

Haley

Until this letter, it had not occurred to me that we have the capacity to give, receive, and feel love from vast distances. When I closed my eyes and simply thought about Haley sitting in her room in the middle of Paris, I realized I required no letter to remind me of our bond, the letter merely evoked a feeling that was already latent and existing. And, while I could point to Paris on a map, and note that Paris is where Haley theoretically *was*, I could still sense her friendship, could physically *feel* and experience her, loving me from afar.

Haley was so far away from all of us, and of course we all felt her absence at the funeral for she was one of us. But from so far away and on a single sheet of paper she taught me that though I may never be able to point to my father's exact location upon a map the way I could so easily point to Paris, this sensation of remote loving was no different. Haley could not attend the funeral and subsequent bizarre festivities, but she *palpably* helped me, from afar. I felt her love. And knew she could feel mine. Why should it be any different with Papa?

For this reason, Haley's letter is now framed and has been in the foyer of every home I have ever occupied in my adult life.

Forever and ever.

Baby Steps

"Dr. Marvin. You can help me.
For the first time in my life, I feel like there's hope."
—*What About Bob?*

It was one to three weeks on . . . give or take . . . about a month after the funeral, and *What About Bob?* was on.

Of course. It had been on, solidly, for a week.

The scene on the screen was Bob and Dr. Marvin's first psychotherapy session in Dr. Leo Marvin's fancy midtown Manhattan office. The office is stuffy despite its large window overlooking the city, cramped with heavy metallic lamps, awards on the wall, and a large bronze bust of Dr. Sigmund Freud. After listening to Bob Wiley—his newest patient—for only a matter of minutes, Dr. Marvin interrupts him:

DR. MARVIN: Bob, there is a groundbreaking new book that has just come out–ah!

Dr. Marvin selects one from dozens of copies of the same, completely visible, book.

DR. MARVIN: Now not everything in this book, of course, applies to you, but I'm sure that you can see, when you see the title, exactly how it could . . . help.
BOB: *Baby Steps?*
DR. MARVIN: It means setting small, reasonable goals for yourself, one day at a time. One tiny step at a time.

BOB: *(wonderstruck)* Baby steps.

DR. MARVIN: For instance, when you leave this office, don't think
      about everything you have to do in order to get out of the building.
      Just think of what you must do to get out of this room, and when
      you get to the hall, deal with that hall, and so forth. You see?

BOB: Baby steps!

DR. MARVIN: Baby steps.

BOB: Oh boy . . .

Baby steps. Agonizingly accurate for me at that moment.

Grey had moved the television from the master bedroom into the upstairs
office across the landing. The master bedroom had a kind of force field
around it—invisible and not discussed. I think all of us were aware that
we did not want to be those people who got all histrionic about the loss of
a loved one—as if that were somehow not acceptable. How many feelings
should we have, exactly? How many feelings should we refrain from feeling? Or, how many should we feel, but refrain from outright displaying?

Mom and I spent a lot of time wondering if we were reacting "normally." Grey, Lilly, and Kent spent a lot of time wondering the same
thing. What do you do when you are eighteen and nothing this devas-
tating has really ever happened to you yet? You can't say things are OK,
or allowed, or understandable because you have no idea if they are or
they aren't—you are eighteen. You are a child. The closest you have ever
gotten to death is the class guinea pig dying in kindergarten. You do not
yet realize what you do not yet know.

So, in that vein, we did not actively close off the Room of Death. No.
We just operated under a silent agreement that all would be quiet. We'd
keep it light. We could and would pretend that all comings and goings to
and from the Room of Death were no big thing. *Look at me, Death*, our
silent attitude declared. *Check me! Check me as I casually use the Master*

Bathroom as a legitimate alternative to other household bathrooms! I am
using it because there is a shower/bath, and because it is a valid option
and therefore should be utilized as such. The "someone died here five
minutes ago" thing? Yeah. It is no big thing.

But it was.

It was a very big thing.

It remained untouched.

Kent and Mom's friend Nancy had gotten to work on the master bathroom (or the Bathroom of Death, if you will),[18] sorting through every pill,
tube, catheter, plug, prescription bottle, and machine before throwing all
of it away without a great deal of ceremony.

"We disposed of the disease," Kent said after returning from wherever these trinkets had been discarded. "We left the man." And indeed,
the gold watch, the spare loose coins he always counted as he thought
and calmed himself, the scraps of paper covered in his signature all-caps
scrawl, the distinctive cologne that smelled so much of him that it pierced
directly into my heart—they were all still there.

Those days were full of harrowing little tasks like that, and I was glad
I didn't have to do them alone.

The death sheets were cleaned and folded, the bed made anew, the
room scrubbed down, the machines carted away—as if none of it had
ever happened at all. Mom's friends, along with mine, took on the duties
that would eventually create the House of Death we came to know after
the death itself was long in the past. All that could remind us of the horrors of terminal disease remained in our memories alone.

But the absence of objects is also a kind of silence. No one could have
prepared us for the pulsing soundlessness that pervaded every waking
moment, that the lack of Michael, along with the lack of his artifacts
(both of the life and the lack-of-life variety) would in fact leave us with no
touchstones for our anguish, no tools with which to dig out the emotions
trapped so deep within us.

Dad's office across the hall already had a small twin bed in the corner

---

18   And I hope you will.

and was now doubling as what could only be described as "Mom's Temporary Place of Sleeping."

At the time, we had one of those late-nineties TVs with a built-in VHS player. It would swallow the already war-worn copy of *Bob*, and every time it reached the end of the tape it would automatically rewind, eject, and the VHS tape would sit in the open mouth of the TV, awaiting instruction—a blank face with its tongue sticking out.

Before a second of silence could go by I would panic, rushing to the machine to push the cassette back in. There are no words to describe how much I loved the way it swallowed the tape with such efficient, satisfying obedience, and I adored the sound of the predigital cogs churning within, of each electronic stage it took to bring Bob's infinite wisdom back to me again.

> **DR. MARVIN:** Are you married?
> **BOB:** I'm divorced.
> **DR. MARVIN:** Would you like to talk about that?
> **BOB:** There are two types of people in this world: Those who like Neil
> Diamond, and those who don't. My ex-wife loves him.

And again. Bob, with his judicious ability to ask for exactly what he needs:

> **BOB:** (*to man on bus*) Hi, I'm Bob. Would you knock me out, please?
> Just hit me in the face . . .

And again. Bob, knowing there is soundness even in folly.

> **DR. MARVIN:** I want some peace and quiet!
> **BOB:** Yeah, I'll be quiet.
> **SIGGY:** I'll be peace!

(*Bob and Siggy burst into giggles.*)

And again. The film, speaking the truth directly to me:

DR. MARVIN: Why are you always wearing black? What is it with you
    and this death fixation?
SIGGY: Maybe I'm in mourning for my lost childhood . . .

It was in this period that I came to know *What About Bob?* beyond
reason or sanity. In that week, I did not laugh at all. I watched this seemingly light, harmless comedy not only because it comforted me; I watched
it because it reminded me of life before this moment. I came to see that
the characters in it were somehow speaking to me, reaching through the
screen and talking directly to me.

Bob on endless loop. Bob, as comforting as any friend or food or love.

I would jolt on occasion when I heard his voice. Dad and Bill Murray
always shared a similar kind of cadence, particularly when Bill Murray
went into his "childlike comedy" mode.

"Ha!" Bob would burst out, and I would jolt upward, certain Dad was
back before I remembered and sank back into myself, and the bed, once more.

If I kept it on, somehow Dad would come around the corner any
second and join me.

After a few days, Fran Steinman came by. She stood over me and
glanced over my particular state of wretchedness and tried to hide how
much the sight of my despair turned her stomach. She caught herself
mid-shudder and plastered a frighteningly cheerful smile on her face. "I
see we are doing a little too much sitting in this bed and not enough getting on with things," she said.

My eyes moved toward her but my body remained motionless, too
dazed to be embarrassed. My eyes peeled away from her and back toward
the screen like a mud-soaked sloth, not even daring to respond. She sighed
and left the room, unable to stir me.

She was trying to help.

Was she trying to tell me that my love of Bob was wrong?

Because if Bob was wrong, then I didn't want to know what right was.

( )

I woke with a start. I had been in the bed for a week. Pajamas filthy, hair matted, and Bob on a bender of inexhaustible reruns.

I did not know what time it was. I did not know the day. All I knew was that it was dark. In every sense. And that I was alone.

But Bob was there, and the blue flame from the small television flickered, more comforting than a fire.

I opened my eyes to discover Bob helping little Siggy dive.

My beloved Bob approached the dock to discover Siggy, dressed fully in black and all alone, sitting on an upright wooden post, red bicycle discarded beside him, despondently playing a hand-held video game. Dr. Marvin insisted that Siggy learn to dive despite Siggy's paralyzing fear of the water. Early in the movie, Dr. Marvin spied Bob sailing past him on a boat with Dr. Marvin's daughter, and in the shock, accidentally dropped Siggy in the water without warning.

Bob was elated, having just returned from his first experience of sailing, and was still draped in his orange life vest that he left casually untied atop his bright blue shirt that read "Don't Hassle Me, I'm Local."

Bob gazed upon Siggy and approached slowly.

BOB: Notice anything different about me?

SIGGY: (*he contemplates Bob for a moment*) No.

BOB: Do you sail?

SIGGY: No.

BOB: Well I just picked it up. Heh! (*He chuckles.*) Wonder what I'm gonna pick up next?

SIGGY: Try diving. (*He retorts sarcastically, returning to his video game.*)

BOB: Alright, diving . . .

SIGGY. I know a great teacher. (*He sighs. Considers for a moment, before venting a confession to Bob.*) I mean, my dad just dropped me in the water. Without warning me first. I mean, I nearly drowned! My whole life passed before my eyes.

BOB: You're lucky you're only twelve.

SIGGY: It was still grim.

I knew exactly what he meant.

SIGGY: I mean what is it with him and diving? What's the big deal?

BOB: Well . . . (*Bob walks out further onto the dock and sees the depth of the water.*) Whoa . . . (*He ties his life vest on tightly before continuing.*) He probably just wants you to beat it, that's all. You know, he probably just wants you to dive, because you're afraid of diving.

(*Siggy rolls his eyes as only a twelve-year-old can, but knows Bob is right.*)

BOB: Did I tell you? I sailed on my first try! (*Bob throws his arms in the air, congratulating himself like a proud child.*) I just let the boat do the work, that was my secret. But with diving, what's the thing? What's the trick?

SIGGY: I dunno. It's supposed to be easy . . .

(*Bob moves his feet around, like a nervous foal.*)

BOB: Well . . . can you give me a handle on it?

(*Siggy puts down his video game and comes over to Bob at the end of the dock.*)

BOB: Thanks.

Moments later? Siggy dives. And he dives because Bob helps him. Does Bob realize he is helping? I don't know. Every time I see this scene, I change my mind. Sometimes I think Bob is innocent; he doesn't know he is the most profound man alive, an all-knowing guru of almost spiritual depth. The next time I watch it, I think, *Yes, Bob knows what he is doing. He may not be able to help himself, but he can help this little boy.* Then back again. And again. I don't know.

I like that I don't know.

What I do know is this: Siggy faces his greatest fear. And he does because Bob helps him.

I burst into tears, which was odd, because I had not yet cried. Not once.

And there I was weeping into the strange unused cushions of an unfamiliar bed in my father's old office, across the hall from the room in which he had died what felt like both moments and ages ago, and all I wanted was for Bob to reach through the screen and help *me*.

The State of Things

Dad thought that the Silbers would look after us. Turns out, Dad was not just wrong, he was dead wrong. Also? Dead.

Now, I cannot say exactly what happened. Partially because I can only suppose I was deemed too young to be told everything. Partially because I (along with my diabolical eulogy) was more than likely a large part of the quarrel. Partially because I was incredibly disinterested. Partially because what I do know and understand is not entirely my story to tell.

But let us suffice it to say the following: I never saw the Silbers again.

There were strongly worded messages, hearsay passed on by innocent casualties stuck in the middle of our cold war, and there was a great deal of flat-out appalling behavior. Yet, even though Mom wracked her brains for understanding, wept over the Silbers for a thousand infuriating reasons, even though we flung our arms upward wondering whether or not this was a *Friday the 13th* movie or possibly *Communist China*, we never found the logic behind the Silbers. We were left only to accept. As in any arms race, the first casualty is sanity.

Perhaps this silent vacuum of guilt-laden non-communication is what Bob might refer to as "isolation therapy." He might concede that the telephone was most likely disconnected. In this particular circumstance, Bob might suggest trying another telephone altogether.

There are some key points to understand:

Mom, Dad and I moved to Michigan in 1993, initially to escape the general collapse of Los Angeles (which felt particularly uncertain after the earthquakes and Rodney King riots), and, to start a new life pegged on the hopes of a potential business deal. Once we arrived, however, the potential business unfortunately dried up. We found ourselves rooted in Michigan with no concrete prospects. Despite the merger debacle years prior, Edna suggested Michael stay and join the family business—begging Michael to stay because Albert was "old and failing" and convincing Albert it was "Michael's duty as the oldest son." Within a year, my father had been diagnosed with cancer.

If the only energetic currency one has is money, it has the power to strike panic into the hearts of those who crave the currency of your love. Withheld cash becomes equal to withheld love.

When Michael earned commissions on business dealings, Albert would begrudgingly pay them out to Michael by deducting them from Michael's "inheritance ledger"—a log he kept for all his decedents. Upon my father's death, Albert was not legally obligated to leave our family anything. My father had given the last years of his life working to enhance the business but Albert unceremoniously absorbed his son's share. Once Michael died, it was as if he had never existed, nor did we.

Without the inheritance of his piece of the family business that my father had anticipated we would receive, my mother and I were left with my father's life insurance policy (a small sum, as life insurance is grim picking for the terminally ill) and the value of our house. There was little else. It required us to be extremely frugal, but we made the most of it.

We did, however, receive a whopping $250! Mom, Kent, and I made our way to the secretary of state office on Telegraph Road in Southfield to present Dad's death certificate and collect his social security. The secretary of state in Michigan is where all voting, organ donation, automotive, and general legal business is sorted out—like a giant waiting room in Purgatory, soft rock blaring, fluorescently lit, and covered in lines.

No, we thought. *Absolutely not, this cannot be.* We looked about us and shook our heads as one always does in any government-related or public-service office. *Where's the express line? Where's the drive-thru? Where is the line for people that are suffering the loss of a loved one?*

Just like at the post office, no one ever budgets their time correctly at the secretary of state. Everyone always assumes it'll be an in-and-out trip, even though it's never been an in-and-out trip, not once. For anyone. *I just want to mail this box from this part of Michigan to another part of Michigan. Where's the line for that?* You are in that line, bitch, and the people behind the counter don't give a shit. *Hi*, they silently say with their flaming red eyes of indifference as you approach, *I'm the only one on the planet who can sort out your future, and it is not a priority for me.*

When we realized that the line we were in was The Line, we knew we would have to wait in this line for longer than we could ever have anticipated. In fact, it was a good thing we were holding Dad's death certificate, because if we all died there too, at least they would know which funeral home to call.

After three hours of waiting, Mom and I presented Dad's death certificate, and we were informed that because my father was twelve years older than my mother, she was too young to collect his social security yet. Mom would get to collect that in over a decade. But that's OK, because today they did have a $250 death package from the government for us. As a consolation. I will continue to deny that on the way out of the secretary of state office I attempted to violently shake some money loose from the pay phones.

With my father's family out of the picture and my mother estranged from her own dysfunctional family, we were left to our own devices.

Except we weren't totally on our own.

There was Kent.

And Grey.

And Lilly.

And a house full of memories.

Only Connect

On the news, everyone was still talking about September 11.
I hated September 11.

I didn't hate it just because it was the most despicable, horrifying act of terrorism in recent American history (though of course that, too). I hated it because I was jealous. The victims' families had the sympathy of the entire world while my father's funeral barely made the obituary section of the *Detroit News*. And I envied them.

I know that it's a terrible, inhumane thing to admit. The whole world was coming apart, yes, but our world was coming apart, too.

But it's true. In my selfish, grieving, eighteen-year-old heart, I was infuriated that it was everywhere.

If I had been a victim of that horrible day I'd be infuriated too: I would have wanted people to stop talking about America and start talking about how my loved one was actually dead. Children wouldn't know their parents. Husbands and wives separated in death by an act of incomprehensible extremism. The back of America had been broken, another age of innocence, lost.

People were dead, and I was jealous. In the most repugnant way. Because all there was in my world was silence.

One of the things no one ever tells you about death is how awkward it is after the first week. You have counted off an entire week of days one by one, and have most likely been swept into a flurry of activity surrounding memorials and relatives and been distracted by that flurry—making plans and picking people up from airports and cleaning your home so that people can see how clean your bathroom is in your darkest hour.

Then there is the tsunami of flowers, donations, dishes of casserole, plus the cards and phone calls (all ranging from the shallowest to the deeply felt). There was what seemed to be a state park forest of trees planted in Dad's name in places we'd never heard of, and, if you can believe it, even a small, terribly special collection of sympathy *e-mails*.[19] While staring at a swimsuit competition-style lineup of fruit baskets, I was an emotional fruit basket.

Ten days after the funeral, the food and cards and letters and trees being planted in Wherever, America, all stopped coming. The fruit baskets began to rot. Borscht went bad in the refrigerator. The mail returned to its normal flow of bills and unsolicited advertisements. The mailbox would open and all one could hear was the crashing silence of other people moving on.

But then came the letter from Judy Chu.

Well into my senior year at Interlochen, I had been presented with a problem—I needed another liberal arts credit in order to graduate with highest academic honors and, as a fully fledged perfectionist, I wasn't about to let three intense acting scenes, a budding secret romance, or a father with cancer stand in my way. I reported to the admissions office to comb through my options.

The options were sparse.

"What about Psychological Lit?" I asked the counselor, Kelly.

"Full." she replied.

"Political Process?"

"You already took it," she said, narrowing her eyes at me.

"What is available?" I asked desperately.

"British Literature," Kelly said, smiling broadly at my predicament.

---

19   Note to everyone: never send a sympathy email. Or, for that matter, a sympathy text.

The world was ending.

British literature? Was this a joke? I envisioned weeks of irritatingly quippy Austen and dreary Brontë passages ahead of me—weeks upon weeks of discussing "the colonies," impending marriage proposals, unexpressed emotions and the *weather*. Christ. I couldn't cope. I buried my head in my hands and realized this was not only my fate but my fault.

"Who teaches it?" I inquired, hoping the answer would improve things—perhaps my favorite teacher taught it and I simply didn't know it.

"Judy Chu."

Who on earth was Judy Chu?

Judy Chu, as it turned out, was a young, energetic, yearlong adjunct teacher from Southern California, brought in to cover for a liberal-arts teacher on sabbatical.

"The students really loved her first semester," Kelly explained. "Her classes are very exciting. Enrollment is light because so many of you want to take the 'greatest hits' before you graduate—but you are a bit late to the party. Obviously."

"Obviously," I said.

I signed up and left the admissions office in a mood, reporting to third-period British Lit the following morning, to a class of only eight other people, most of whom were procrastinators just like me.

Judy Chu began with a bright smile, and asked each of us why we had enrolled in British Literature.

Dear God, I thought, not wanting to admit the truth, and I think I squeezed past the issue by explaining that fate had brought me here.

But fate had indeed brought me to Judy Chu. Her class became the most important literary experience of my life.

This thoughtful young teacher was tough but fair, with complex weekly handouts and uncompromising standards for grammar, essay construction, and literary criticism. Plus, I can honestly say she taught me everything I've nearly forgotten about punctuation, verb tenses, and second-person voice.

But nothing will ever expunge the greatest lesson and gift she gave me: Judy Chu taught me how to read, and perhaps more crucially, why. Lady Chu (which I named her myself, for she is a lady first, if you ask me) was bibliophilic magic. She handed you a book and ostensibly gave you magical incantations that allowed you to leap inside the pages—like the children in *Mary Poppins* jumping inside Bert's sidewalk chalk painting. That final semester of high school was just the beginning.

When she assigned *Howards End*, she blew my literary mind. The copy still sits proudly on my bookshelf adorned with well-thumbed pages, color-coded highlighting, and adorable teenaged margin notes (such as "Love is a 'He?'" and "When you show your homeland to a foreigner how do you show it all?" and "Oh . . . more LIFE!" and, of course, "Is love the only way to connect?"). I can still remember how much I grew to love it more with every turn of the page. The deeply feeling narrator (perhaps the voice of Forster himself), the poetry in the slightest of prose, the humanity, and of course, my beloved kindred spirit—*Howards End*'s heroine, Margaret Schlegel. With every word Margaret uttered, my heart leapt in recognition, for Margaret Schlegel lived in me—her flaws, her resilience, her optimism, and her heart. I had never identified with a character like this before, and it was because Judy Chu showed me how to personalize literature.

At the end of the year, Judy Chu bid Interlochen farewell, but not before leaving our tiny class with one final handout. The simple sheet of white paper quoted Mary Oliver's "Wild Geese" and T. H. White's *The Book of Merlyn* (beckoning us to learn) on one side, a personalized note to every one of us on the other. I still have this piece of paper, which held a very simple message:

"Al: You are Margaret Schlegel to me."

A few weeks after my father's death, I stood outside beside the mailbox in clothing I had worn for days. A light rain was spitting down from a sheet-white sky. I pulled from the mailbox a small envelope about the size of my hand with the mark of a black and red Chinese dragon traveling from back to front. I recognized the small, perfectly neat handwriting immediately.

Dear Al, the letter read. *I know that you, with your strong, strong heart, shall see pain through to hope and prosper. With love, Judy Chu*

I held the letter to my heart. It said so little and meant so much. I wrote back to say so. It would be the first of a lifetime of letters. Letters to and from Judy Chu to every single address I would ever have in my adult life.

The Walk from 1367

Here is how you take The Walk.

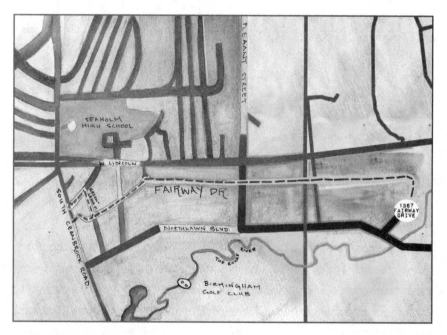

1. Head Northeast on Fairway toward Pleasant Street. (Take a look
   to your right and behold the long line of hanging American flags
   that adorn almost every home on the street, all the way down to
   the Presbyterian and Methodist churches on Maple Road).

2. Continue to follow Fairway Drive past Golfview Boulevard, pass by Greenlawn Street. (Do say hello to passersby, especially Don and his dog Daisy at the top of the hill).

3. Turn right onto South Cranbrook Road. (The street is very busy here, so feel free to walk on the incredibly large lawns of one or more of the neighbors.)

4. Turn right and loop onto Greenlawn Street, then get back onto Fairway. Or, alternatively, if you are feeling frisky, walk all the way to West Lincoln, pass Seaholm High School, and reconnect with Fairway at Pleasant Street. (Don't miss the absolutely beautiful garden of the elderly woman with the Dalmatian tucked away behind Hillside, or the dreamlike barn house with the bright green door that must belong to a growing family).

5. Enjoy the walk back down Fairway (which is entirely downhill), especially in the early morning or as the sun is setting.

6. Round the Rouge River Park as you reach the home stretch.

7. Turn left into the driveway.

8. You are home.

This was the walk my family took almost every day of our lives since the time we moved to 1367 during the summer of 1994. We'd head up the hills after summer meals; we'd trudge through snow and leaves and rain. My parents would discuss the world, and we'd sing and laugh and greet our neighbors as they passed. The childless German couple down the street threw an Oktoberfest gathering that included beer and an actual appearance of lederhosen. The aloof couple next door with their pack of adopted greyhounds. Tom and Sal became the first gay couple on the street when they moved into the corner house with their beloved dog Riley. Bill and his beautiful baritone voice and love of classic radio lived with his wife Pat and their flurry of offspring on the kitty-corner. Dick and Anne lived directly across the street; Dick was gruff on the outside, soft within, Anne a Southern belle. She watched the phones the day we all trudged off to the funeral home declaring in her Virginia drawl "why it would be my absolute pleasure y'all, your father once kissed me on the cheek and I blushed because he was so handsome."

The almost frighteningly bright family of four next door with whom we shared so many wonderful dinners. The Kuhnes, who lived around the sharp curve of the street with their two gorgeous daughters we all watched grow up. They moved away in the late nineties, but we never lost touch with them because we continued to check in, laugh, and meet for dinner in our very own downtown Birmingham. My neighbors on Fairway Drive—we used to get together for picnics and barbecues. We drank sangria in our backyards those summer nights, then walked along the River Rouge that flowed behind our houses.

At the end, The Walk was not possible for Dad. Making it to the end of the driveway was a victory. A breathless, crushing victory.

It was on The Walk in the days that followed the funeral that it happened. Mom and I would walk together—both of us closer to the person we had lost and now getting to know one another as if from scratch. All history had been stolen and erased, and only on the pavements of Fairway Drive could the stories be rewritten.

On The Walk, I truly got to know my mother.

"Tell me a story from your childhood," I would say.

"Why?" she asked.

"Well, I suppose because I would like to know about when you were little. I bet you were very cute."

"I was cute."

Cute! We were getting somewhere!

"I can see it: little tiny Cathy, all cute in her perfect dress with her beautiful Californian life, you must have great stories!"

Mom kept her pace and her gaze straight ahead on the horizon. Her face did not change a bit. "I don't," she said.

"You don't what?"

"I don't have great stories."

"Oh," I said, irritated that I had hit a wall. "Well, why not?"

"I don't really remember," she answered.

I was incredulous.

"You don't remember *anything* about your childhood?" I asked derisively.

"Not really," she said. "Just little things here and there. Like flashing snips of a film reel."

"Well, what about something from my childhood, then?"

Mom looked thoughtful for a moment. Then she said, her voice a little stronger, "Do you remember your fourth birthday?"

I did. For my fourth birthday, I had a classic gymnasium birthday party at local Los Angeles haunt Joey's Gym—a morass of young adults in Lycra leading preschoolers through ball pits and zip lines. I wore a teal leotard, loving every second of my very first "public" birthday party.

We talked about my birthday, and then my mother's story began to trickle in.

When my mother was nearly four years old, she had the first of what would be a lifetime of imaginative bursts. She envisioned a colorful cake for her birthday—with all the colors, lights, and sounds of a carnival carousel. This "carousel cake" was dreamed about, hoped for, and wished upon stars for, taking shape in her little mind.

At long last, the day arrived. When the song began and the cake came out, Cathy's heart leapt, then instantly broke. The cake placed before her had a crude collection of cheap straws and animal crackers, all supposedly meant to represent a carousel. She had never been more devastated in all her life, and without meaning to, Cathy broke down into fat, silent tears.

Cathy's mother feigned amusement at Cathy's tears for the guests, but after the guests left, the floodgates holding back her fury broke. She railed at Cathy for being "difficult." Cathy was silent and still as her mother punished her, then finally asked the real matter of her upset. "It was just not how I saw it in my imagination," Cathy had said. It was not that she was ungrateful. It had nothing to do with being spoiled. Cathy had a fantasy in her head she desperately wanted to be real.

"Ungrateful girl," her mother hissed, and Cathy was sent to bed.

( )

My mother was the daughter of Colleen Mary Malloy, an up-and-coming mezzo-soprano with the Los Angeles Opera. A local beauty, Colleen was the eldest of five in the Irish Catholic Malloy family. She had always been prone to bouts of temper, drama, and fly-in-the-face rebellion. Perhaps that is why she married Delalberto Noriega, who was home from the army, and serving as an airplane mechanic—a man cursed with the worst last name and cultural makeup possible in 1940s Southern California.

Against her parents' wishes, Colleen temporarily abandoned her opera ambitions when she married Delalberto (the Malloys, in fact, refused to attend the wedding). But she went about rebelliously playing house regardless (though whether she did so out of cultural pressure, dissidence, or fear I suppose no one will ever know).

They lived in a house in Norwalk, California, with a white-picket fence and a large backyard. During that time, Delalberto was called to Alaska to work on a building project, leaving Colleen to take care of their two young children—my mother Catherine and her older brother Charlie—on her own.

One day, a traveling Jewel Tea salesman knocked on their door. Not just a humble salesman, this Jewel Tea man had a vast knowledge of opera and seduction. Colleen was smitten. Before long, she piled her children in the car in the middle of the night and they woke up the next morning in Texas, hoping to start a new life with the Jewel Tea salesman who was surprised to see that their affair had inspired such a drastic action.

It would be the first of many troubles.

By the time Delalberto returned to Los Angeles, Colleen had too—without the Jewel Tea salesman, but with one foot out the door and asking for a divorce.

In those days, it was almost unheard of in California for children of divorce to be awarded to anyone but the mother's care, so at four and five years old, off Cathy and Charlie went with their impulsive mother, to what would become a series of apartments, co-ops, opera digs, boy-friends' houses, and strangers' spare rooms.

"You would think that having a beautiful opera diva for a mother would be magical," Mom once told me. "But it wasn't."

Mom would never go into too much detail about that part of her life. She could not remember. Or would not. Perhaps a bit of both. A blank darkness had blocked a great deal of it out.

Because life with her mother was terrifying.

Charlie was always Colleen's "little man," but Cathy only seemed to evoke jealousy from Colleen, despite showing many signs of having inherited her mother's artistic gifts. Still, both children were left largely neglected.

There aren't many photographs of Charlie and Cathy from that time. The ones that do exist of these "Irish twins" are startling: two smiling, bright-eyed children, desperately close and marked with a unique beauty that came from the collision of their parents' ethnic backgrounds. They are also gaunt. Not the lean, appealing Californian postwar look of scrawny youths in a constant state of growth. No. These children are starving, their flesh too flimsy for their frames, their bones sticking out unnaturally. Colleen did not have food in the house. She often forgot to feed them. So they went unfed.

Radical characters in the shape of friends, artistic colleagues, lovers, and everything in between flew in and out of their various homes, staying long into the night and sometimes into the following morning. One day, after months of strange behavior and tented outfits, nine-year-old Cathy returned from school to find her mother gone, informed she would return in a couple of days. It was not until years later that Cathy would realize her mother had given birth to the love child of an Algerian baritone she had met at the Golden Earring—a wild bohemian haunt in Los Angeles where 1950s opera wannabes would go and perform to feel important.

Colleen had given the baby up at the hospital before casually returning home as if nothing had happened.

Every few weeks, there was a new male companion, far too many of whom—or so I have deduced from scraps of what Cathy has told me over the years—did unnamable things to Colleen's young daughter.

In 1961, at eleven and twelve years old, Cathy and Charlie were asked to testify against their mother in a precedent-setting trial that would decisively take away Colleen's custody rights and attracted a great deal of local attention. Full custody was awarded to their father Delalberto Noriega, who had remarried a wonderful woman named Florence; both of them had been fighting for Delaberto's kids for years.

Cathy and Charlie never saw their mother again.[20]

"Want to do this again tomorrow?" Mom asked as we made our way up the path to our front door.

"Sure," I nodded.

We would not do it every day.

It would not be easy. But each walk was a few steps closer to growing closer.

---

20 Before this case, sole paternal custody had never before been awarded to the father in California.

Green Grow the Lilacs or,
A *Brief Non Sequitur of Vital Import*

Where most families might have friendly game night gathered casually around a Trivial Pursuit board, or outwit one another about history or sports trivia, the Silbers had an ongoing Theater Factoid Quiz Bowl. My father, a man with a seemingly infallible knowledge of everything, served as Alex Trebek-style Quiz Master extraordinaire.

"Which Academy Award-winning actress originated the role of Sally Bowles in London?"

"Judi Dench!" we would yell in unison.

"Bonus question: in which theater?"

"The Palace!"

We would read plays, devour films, documentaries, and, of course, sing along to musicals in the car.

When I was twelve, my very first truly meaningful theatrical experience was playing Louise, daughter of the ne'er-do-well carnival barker Billy Bigelow, in a community theater production of *Carousel*. I became so enamored with the piece that Dad invested in a giant, encyclopedic Rodgers and Hammerstein coffee-table book. I quickly devoured every page.

One day, my father said, "Isn't it fascinating how the 'musicalization' of a play can sometimes be nearly identical to the source material and how, for others, the musical might not resemble the play material at all, as with *Oklahoma!* and *How Green is My Valley?*"

Record scratch.

My father was never wrong. He was the Ken Jennings to my "Kid's Week" *Jeopardy!* competitor. But today, I knew I had him.

"But Dad," I whispered. "*Oklahoma* isn't based on *How Green is My Valley*. It's based on *Green Grow the Lilacs*."

There was a long pause.

"Oh?" he said.

"Yes." I replied.

"I don't think so . . . " he hesitated.

"I know so!" I exclaimed, running to grab the Rodgers and Hammerstein coffee-table book in victory. "You see?"

Dad glanced the page over and nodded.

"Well noted, Al," he said, smiling. It was the first time anything like that had ever happened.

"Green grow the lilacs" quickly became a family catchphrase, a joke we all merrily joined in on. It came to be a phrase synonymous with "nobody's perfect." Got the wrong apples at the grocery store? Ah well, green grow the lilacs. Bad parallel parking job? Green grow the lilacs.

Two years later, Dad was driving along in the beat-up, silver, late-eighties Oldsmobile his father made him drive to and from all of their various property locations. He was listening to a local radio station which was holding a phone-in contest, offering an incredible prize for anyone who could answer three Broadway trivia questions: an all-expenses paid weekend in New York with two tickets to, of all things, *Ragtime*.

Dad called in.

He answered question one correctly. Question two? Not a problem. And then came question three: "On what play is the musical *Oklahoma!* based?"

Dad grinned from ear to ear. "*Green Grow the Lilacs*!" he exclaimed.

He won.

That was how we all got to New York City to see the original cast of *Ragtime* on Broadway.

He was magic that way.

The Cat

There are some things we just cannot explain.

It was now late October, and it was unseasonably warm for Michigan. The trees, which should have been mostly bare by then, still glittered amber in the glow of the street lights set against the deep cobalt blue of the sky behind them, like pieces in a velvet jewel box. We could feel in our skin that the dew would be heavy in the morning.

Kent and I were on The Walk. Silent and solemn, we strolled hand in hand along the curves and reaches of Fairway Drive, taking in the oddness of warmth in the evening sky, the strange intensity of the colors, and an unshakeable feeling that something was happening. There was mystery in the air; we could feel it in the light, humid breeze.

Kent and I walked on, blanketing ourselves from the evening. Without discussing it, Kent began to sing—quiet and low, light but solid. His voice was distinctive; it cut through the dark as I linked on to the song, my own voice dancing on top and then below, weaving in the harmony that was our specialty.

I'll admit that at the time, I did not possess a particular faith. Prior to that evening, I had never given significant thought to what we'll just call *the world beyond*. I was raised in a largely secular home. I had gone to Jewish preschool and kindergarten. I had played Golde in *Fiddler on the Roof* sophomore year of high school. I had read *Macbeth*, and I knew not to mess with the Ouija board. There was no one to pray to, there was no structured religion to comfort me but an inner self-reliant religion of the spirit. I believed in good and evil. I accepted that good and evil was just how the world worked. I was afraid of unknowns, but I believed everything happened for a reason, and that forces, invisible and unnamable, were at work in the universe.

All at once, there was a gust of wind so strong I buried my face in Kent's chest. He wrapped his arms around me, his own face shielded from the wind within the mass of my hair.

When we looked up, there it was, plain as day.

The cat before us was a silent ginger thing: collarless and almost impossibly orange with white markings on his face and paws and a bright white front that looked as if he were wearing a formal dress shirt. He—for you could just sense that it was a he—sat looking upward, paws together, his tail curled perfectly around his feet. One could not deny—no matter how many times you blinked or shook your head—that he was smiling.

Kent and I stared in silence. We looked at the cat. Then at one another. Was this really happening?

Kent crouched down and reached his hand out toward the cat. *Psssst psst pssssst,* he cooed, rubbing his fingers together, beckoning. The cat walked in a grand circle, making the dramatic entrance of a great actor perfectly catching his light. He approached and nuzzled lovingly into Kent's outstretched hand. Kent smiled and scratched under the cat's ginger jowls, much to their mutual pleasure.

Soon the cat caught my eye and stopped. *What? No nuzzling from you?* his expression said. I hesitated, but leaned down and stroked the cat along the length of his back. He responded differently to my touch, twisting thoughtfully and placing his head in the crook of my elbow. The gesture startled me. I stood, and having seemingly satisfied the cat's needs, quickly backed away and swiftly started making my way home. Kent rushed to catch up with me, taking my hand as we moved through the darkness.

Suddenly, Kent stopped dead in his tracks. "Al . . . " he whispered, looking over my shoulder. I turned.

It was the cat. It was following us home.

We opened the door to 1367, eyes locked on the cat. He hesitated only a moment before walking inside.

"What's going on?" said Mom, sensing something as she came upstairs to the foyer. Catching sight of the cat, she gasped.

"Who is this?" she asked.

We made way for the cat as he slowly surveyed the entire house, placing his paw contemplatively upon the walls, nuzzling up against the corners, soaking the place in. He ran downstairs, then thundered upstairs to peak into the office, the bathroom, my bedroom. Finally, he stood before the entrance of the master bedroom. He stared through the door left ajar—absolutely still, not breathing, not twitching, frozen in a kind of resolve.

He entered.

He jumped up onto the Bed of Death, circled the side that days ago had been Michael's, and settled into the spot, head down, eyes closed.

The three of us had followed the cat throughout his house tour and now we lingered in the doorway, mouths agape.

"Mike?" Kent said. It was as if the word fell out of his mouth without the will of the speaker.

The cat opened his eyes, lifted his head, and stared directly at me.

Suddenly he bolted beneath the bed, struggled with an invisible adversary, screeching, mewing, and without any warning, thundered down the stairs and out the still-open front door, never to be heard from again. Like a comet, one moment vivid and dazzling, the next vanished, away on its own journey through the endless dark unknown.

The following night, I dreamed: Dad was back, and no one thought it was peculiar or remarkable but me. I made my way upstairs and a particularly well-fed, healthy-looking Dad was leaving the shower in his favorite green velour bathrobe. I did a double take, stopping him on the landing with sheer joy.

"Dad," I cried. "Oh Dad, you're back!"

"Hi, Al," he said, smiling hugely, neither confirming nor denying my previous statement. "It's good to see you."

"Oh, yes!" I could not stare at him hard enough, could not suck in enough of his smell that was so pungent. Tears fill my eyes. "Papa, we've all missed you."

He nodded and, with only the slightest tinge of sadness, he gathered his green robe close around himself and moved to make his way up the stairs.

"Wait! Dad!" I said. I had to know. "The cat."

He smiled.

"The cat, Papa. Was—was that . . . ?"

Dad came down a few steps and got as close to me as I could sense he was "allowed." He laughed a little.

"Of course," he said, eyes sparkling, "but you knew that."

I nodded.

"I knew you'd be afraid of a ghost or an angel, anything like that. I knew you would need to know that you had seen it, touched it. And I just had to make certain everything was OK." He turned to go again.

"Wait—Papa!" I cried, not wanting him to go just yet. "Please. What's it like?"

"Al . . . " he sighed. "You know I can't answer that."

I nodded again.

He turned to go again, but stopped himself. Then, looking down at me, he said, "It's everything you hope it is."

I woke in tears. Comforted, but certain of nothing. Certain only that we know nothing about the world beyond.

So why not believe? Because it happens. These things do. Happen.

The Bed of Death

A week or so after the incident with the cat, Grey headed home for Thanksgiving, slated to return to his creative den (in our downstairs spare bedroom) as soon as possible to continue work on his theatrical set-design model for his college *re*-applications.

As previously discussed, Lilly was the only one of us that returned to college that year, and, despite her frequent commutes up and down I-75 in her pale-blue Dodge caravan to visit "Cathy and the drop outs" at the House of Death, she had to spend *some* time at Oberlin—she had to make friends and make reeds and, to quote Grey, "do Oboe stuff." As our sole remaining higher education ambassador, Kent, Grey and I mined her constantly for tales of college life—from bulk cooking for her campus commune, to her sudden and inexplicable joining of the Oberlin Aikido Club.[21] Though Lilly insisted the Oberlin was like Interlochen for college students (even going so far as to call it *"Oberlochen"*) to us, Lilly's Freshman year all sounded like some sort of Liberal Arts Safari, complete with tales of normal eighteen-year-old college students grazing and mating in their natural habitat.

Two critical characters down and left to our own devices, Kent suggested it might be time to start thinking about changing the Room of Death.

---

21   Another use of the 1997 pale blue Dodge caravan was hauling the Aikido Club on a trip to Cincinnati.

"A new bed for sure," he said. "Perhaps some paint, a little classic Cathy DIY?"

"Great idea," Mom said, and, three hours later, Kent and I returned from grocery shopping to find that Mom had discovered beautiful solid hardwood floors beneath the early nineties carpet, ripped all of it up, rolled it up, and taken it out to the curb. She had finished the bedroom and was already hard at work on the hallway, breathless, sweating, and determined. All of this served to reaffirm a notion I already knew about Cathy—once you put an idea in her head, there's no stopping her.[22]

The three of us spent the remainder of the night ripping up that hideous beige carpet and hauling it out to the curb. By 3 a.m., we had disposed of the detritus of our former life upon the edges of our lawn and were filled with an odd sense of higher purpose. We were not scavengers rummaging through the ruins of a fallen city; We were excavators! Like Heinrich Schliemann! Below the carpets lay new, undiscovered Troys and we would be the team to peel away the rubble, reveal the past, and simultaneously uncover the future—just like the archeologists of yore!

When we woke the following morning, the artifacts were gone, taken to the same unnamable place to which all life's mysteries disappear.

But we were not empty, we were lighter somehow.

The top floor of 1367 had been stripped bare to make room for new life, and we dressed that morning with a purpose.

We were going to buy a new bed.

Art Vann on Woodward at Fourteen Mile was the first and only option that sprang to mind. We knew the name well from near-constant radio and local television commercials, and besides, it was on the same strip of Woodward as Dairy Deluxe, which gave it street cred (not to mention zero percent financing until 2004).

We arrived to find that Art Vann was above a Mercedes dealership. To enter, one had to ascend in an escalator that crested onto a cavernous warehouse floor of fluorescently lit sofas, dinettes, media stations, and bed frames.

---

22   Do not get between my mother and a power tool.

Mom, Kent, and I were each splayed snow-angel style on a series of mattresses, gazing upward at the humming lights.

"Too firm over here," Kent called out. "It's a Sealy."

"Al?"

"S'OK. A bit squishy."

"I'm on one of those individual coil ones over here," Mom said, "the one from that commercial with the glass of wine and the bowling ball."

"Oh yeah!"

"How is it?"

"It's great. It's just right."

Just then Mort, a stout middle-aged gentleman whose comb-over, jacket, smile, and every gesture indicated that he was an Art Vann salesman, leaned over into my vision and, hands clasped behind his back, asked, "Anything I can do for you?"

"We were just waiting for our porridge to cool," I said.

"We'll take this one," Mom said.

Throw in three bowls of porridge and a blonde girl, and we'd have had ourselves a fairy-tale ending.

"Excellent," said Mort, straightening up, eyeing us still. "You're certain of the queen?"

"No doubt about the queen," Kent smiled at Mom. We had decided that downsizing from the king-sized Death Bed felt right.

"And we'll take this frame," said Mom. "I like it— it looks like a sleigh."

It did—a chestnut, caramel-stained, queen-sized sleigh.

"I'll draw up the papers," said Mort, as he turned on his tiny feet, hands still behind his back.

As Mort trotted away, we turned to Mom, who was deep in thought.

"A new bed . . . " I said.

"Yes," she said, running her hand along the hip of the frame.

"Happy?" Kent asked in a low voice.

Mom thought a moment before answering. Of course she was not happy. Her one and only love was gone—gone almost as callously as the upstairs carpets. The Silbers were evil, the government unhelpful, she was lost, abandoned once again, and living in Detroit with a gaggle of equally lost teenagers. It all crossed her mind; you could see it in her face, in the thoughtful hand still caressing the chestnut bed frame.

At last, the hand stopped moving. Mom paused and clutched the wood, felt its solid weight. She focused on the bed—her brand new queen-sized, chestnut sleigh bed, with thick orthopedic mattress, box spring and twenty percent Thanksgiving discount, all fit for a queen.

"Happy," she said.

This was a step—a baby step, as Bob would say—toward the next stage of our new life, and that made her happy.

"Psychic Mike"

It had always been understood that Dad possessed a certain kind of sensitivity. We never used the word "psychic" though; that seemed crass. In fact, we rarely talked about it at all. It merely was, and so we continued our lives, every now and then stippled with an event no one could truly explain.

We would be driving along the highway at night and Dad would drastically slow his speed as we turned a corner, prompting Mom to ask him why.

"There's going to be a deer," Dad would explain. And sure enough, there would be—a large deer standing in the middle of the highway, as if he had been waiting for us. We would remain silent as Dad flickered the headlights to shoo the deer off the road before continuing on, never to speak of it—merely filing it away under "C," for coincidence.

Once, just after we had moved to Michigan, we were having a particularly difficult financial time—the cost of the move from California, his recent health troubles, and a miserable deal Dad had been working on for his father. At breakfast, before everyone headed off, Dad sat hunched sketching on a sheet of paper in a twisted, left-handed stance. He was sketching out a symbol, flecking the page with his pen, brow furrowed.

"What's that?" I asked, looking over with curiosity.

"Something I dreamed," he replied, "it appeared in my dreams over and over again—an unknown, somewhat familiar symbol next to the number four. I wanted to see if I could capture it."

Later that night, hours after Mom had picked me up from school and long after dinner should have been eaten, Dad had not yet returned. Mom gazed out the window of our temporary apartment in Troy, Michigan—where we had lived just before we moved in to 1367—concern clear upon her face. Moments later, Dad walked in the front door, hands stuck firmly in his pockets, face slanted downward, almost as if ashamed.

"Michael where have you been?" Mom cried. "I was worried!"

"I'm sorry," Dad said, voice modest.

"Dad," I said. "What's the matter?"

Dad kept his eyes locked on the ground, his face very grave. "I had to see it through," he declared.

"See what through?" said Mom.

"The symbol from my dream. I had to know what it was and if it meant anything."

Most people would have responded to such a claim by scoffing (or burying their head in their hands, or perhaps by berating the person for being a fool). But not us—we were used to moments such as this. Though we never could have dreamed of what came next.

"It did," Dad whispered, the grave look on his face suddenly filled with sparkle. "I knew I recognized the symbol. It's not something I ever would have thought of had I not had the strongest instinct to take a different road to work today. As I was driving I passed the racetrack, it hit me. That symbol was a betting symbol. I pulled in, parked the car, and put it all on horse number four."

"What?" my mother and I said in unison, dumbstruck. To our knowledge Dad had never bet on horses—or anything at all, for that matter.

At that, Dad's hands flew out of his pockets and into the air he flung thousands of dollars.

We all laughed and cheered and hugged one another amid the wash of money now scattered bountifully throughout our apartment.

It was magical. It was.

But it was not even remotely the most magical thing that had ever happened to the Silber family.

We teemed with magic.

And the magic came from him.

I awake in a sweat. The room smells of his cologne—the one we had boxed away and stored in the garage weeks ago. I am wide awake. I looked about me, eyes sharp, searching for tonight's message.

Then there it was.

In the pool of moonlight flooding in from the bedroom window that overlooks River Rouge, it lays there clear as day: a dollar bill.

Getting Over Your Grief

BOB: Excuse me, Phil, but with these particular symptoms, is Prozac the right choice?

LILY MARVIN: You think Prozac is a mistake?

BOB: Well, with this kind of manic episode, I would think Librium might be a more effective management tool.

DR. PHIL: You could be right. I'll rewrite the prescription.

— What About Bob?

There are few situations on earth more awkward than the aftermath of someone kicking the bucket. As a result, the same paltry bits of advice have been recycled for years to try to save people from embarrassing conversations. Let me assure you: *they do not work.* If and when you find yourself in this unforgiving situation of having recently lost a loved one, you will most likely be met with the following suggestions, in order for those around you to feel more at ease about your constant, stabbing emotional pain.

Inactive? *Why don't you enjoy a nice walk in the woods?* Your friends may suggest.

Can't sleep? *Why don't you put an amethyst under your pillow?*

Join a painting group.

Make some pots.

Snuggle.

You know what I want to say to all of those people? "I'm busy not bathing, not eating, and watching Bill Murray and Nora Ephron movies on repeat and don't care if I smell like a sewer or bike shorts drenched in caustic lye. And speaking of bike shorts, let me tell you where you can put that amethyst . . . "

Prepare yourself for some cold hard truths.

WHAT "THEY" WILL TELL YOU TO DO	AL'S INTERPRETATION OF WHAT "THEY" *REALLY* MEAN:
MEMORIALIZE! Plant a tree, start a fund, or run in a charity race.	If you insist.
JOIN A SUPPORT GROUP. You don't have to be alone with your feelings or your pain.	Wow. Gosh. They—whoever "they" are—just have the best answers to everything. I'm going write "you don't have to be alone with your feelings or your pain" down in my catalog of "Brilliant Things They Said."
EXPRESS YOUR EMOTIONS! Don't stop yourself from having a good cry if you feel one coming on. Watch sad movies, play sad music, and bring back memories of the person that you lost. Feel free!	Do not cry. Tears are icky and make people squeamish. Also, you know who likes tears? Al-Qaeda.
GRIEF IS NORMAL! Time heals all. It'll pass!	Right. And Enola Gay was delivering origami paper.
BE AROUND PEOPLE. Even informal gatherings of family and friends bring a sense of support. They help not to feel so isolated in the first days and weeks of their grief.	What do you call this? What? Does living in the House of Death with my grieving mother and a slew of college dropouts not count for anything anymore?

WHAT "THEY" WILL TELL YOU TO DO	AL'S INTERPRETATION OF WHAT "THEY" *REALLY* MEAN:
TALK ABOUT IT! Some people find it helpful to talk about their feelings. But no one should feel pressured to talk.	Good. Because I think I'll just watch *What About Bob?* on repeat, thanks.
EXPRESS YOURSELF. Even if you don't feel like talking, find ways to express your emotions and thoughts. Journal about memories, and how you're feeling since the passing. Or write a song, poem, or tribute about your loved one and share it with others.	Give this a hard pass. Does anyone here understand that a person has a right not to have their personal life picked apart mercilessly in a public forum? I am not Monica Lewinsky.
EXERCISE. Exercise can help your mood. It may be hard to get motivated, so modify your usual routine if you need to.	Does this include taking boxing? Because I could get really motivated if my exercise regime included the possibility of KO-ing my grandparents. After all, I'm just healing, and healing feels good. Incredibly good—like Christian Bale dressed as he was in Little Women kissing me with a mouth full of Oreos good.
EAT RIGHT. Your body needs fuel.	Thank the Lord above for the invention of the sandwich, and for the fact that Kent makes the best sandwich on earth. Where would we be without the sandwich? You'd have to chug a shot of peanut butter and then desperately chase it with a shot of jelly. You'd pound fistfuls of luncheon meat into your maw and chug Grey Poupon just to feel alive. (There is only so much you can stare at a fridge full of kugel . . .)
RITUALS. Funerals and other memorial traditions help people get through the first few days and honor the person who died.	I think we have previously established that that sucked pretty hard.

Mostly, the reality is that most people want to say, "Get off your ass and stop being sad." But mostly they just tolerate you. And let's face it: there is just nothing better than being tolerated.

*   *

"I feel good, I feel great, I feel wonderful," are the first words of *What About Bob?* Bob Wiley sits on his bed in his hermetically sealed New York apartment, fiercely massaging his temples, repeating his mantra over and over again as he attempts to psych himself up enough to leave the security of his apartment to see Dr. Leo Marvin for the first time. It's a brilliant opener—sardonic, irreverent, and oddly touching all at once.

We recited Bob's opening mantra a lot in those first weeks, massaged our temples and laughed together. The pressure to feel better, move forward, or just simply get any scrap of shit done was looming over us like a personal injury attorney at a highway car accident.

I never returned to the University of Minnesota or the Guthrie Training Program. I only ever returned to Minneapolis to retrieve my things. I returned to my tiny coffin-like single room on the thirteenth floor of the gigantic college dormitory and despite barely knowing them, my classmates were very kind. They helped assemble boxes, fold clothes, and inherited my collegiate dorm-room artifacts. I hugged them all and wished them well.

I returned to Michigan. I was officially a college dropout.

*   *

Here is the schedule:

STEP 1
Late each night, we set a time to wake up the next morning (which we always ignore).

STEP 2

Mom goes to her makeshift office Place of Sleeping in Dad's old office
(the new bed had arrived, but she didn't quite feel ready to sleep in the
room), Kent and I go to my room at the top of the stairs, and Grey goes
to his in the downstairs guestroom.

STEP 3

We yell goodnight.

STEP 4

We sleep.

STEP 5

The next morning, we meet in the kitchen, where Mom and I have coffee
and Grey and Kent have Cheerios. We then go about planning a very precise
schedule that completely falls apart by midmorning. This happens daily.

STEP 6

After the morning gathering, Grey and Kent report to the downstairs
bathroom, emerging twenty to thirty minutes later triumphant, both of
them basking in the glory of their regularity.

STEP 7

We all shower and get dressed for the morning activities. Grey reports to
his cave. I go for a run (because I have, mysteriously, taken up running)
or Mom and I go on The Walk. Kent pours over the political sections of
the paper.

STEP 8

We report back around noon in an attempt to achieve in the day ahead.
This could hold any number of activities, which may or may not include:

- ★ College re-audition preparations (this includes, at first,
  a great deal of time spent on the Internet trying to truly

find places for all of us to *go* to school; then making lists,
gathering audition requirements, and making phone calls;
and eventually filling out applications, working on pieces,
and Grey spending countless hours designing a model set for
the musical *Cabaret* in his guestroom/office/cave).

★ Plans for a DIY revamp of the House of Death
★ A trip to our regular hangout, the place we eat when we
  forget to cook; Greek Islands Coney Restaurant (herein
  known simply by its initials "GI")
★ Reading *Harry Potter* (all of us for the very first time) and
  obsessively talking about it and preparing for the launch
  of the first film. And then following the release of said
  film, obsessing over that, and driving to the Birmingham
  Palladium to watch the movie nearly every day.
★ Local tourism (with visits including the Henry Ford and
  Motown museums and a trip the grounds of the Cranbrook
  House, Gardens, and Science Center.)
★ Planning ahead for Thanksgiving and Christmas and New
  Year.

STEP 9
We either cook dinner or go out to find something to eat.

STEP 10
We do it all over again.

People assume that artists, the self-employed, and college dropouts are no
better than drug dealers and late sleepers—they are obviously lethargic
and worthless and clearly to be lumped in with those miscreants who
party until dawn at a drug-fueled rave, drenched in sweat and glitter with
glow sticks stuffed in their Lycra bras.

We didn't love our existence in those days, but it was what it was:
necessary. We may have been unemployed college dropouts, but we
weren't covered in glitter: we were pitching in. We were discovering the

meaning of life by rebuilding a life, at 1367. Above all, were all finding our way.

We felt good.

We felt great.

We felt wonderful.

Opa

Everyone needs a place like Greek Islands Coney Restaurant.

You know—a local joint that's just the right balance between casual and quality so you never have to worry about whether the food is going to be any good or, critically, what you have to wear. A place where they know your family, your usual, and where "everybody knows your name."

Hand-painted murals grace the walls of Greek Islands. The first (in "section five") is a copy of the ceiling of the Sistine Chapel only God and Adam are reaching for a Coney dog. The other (which blazes just above the entrance) is of the Last Supper painted with Greek gods instead of Christian disciples. I knew every person that bused the tables, waited them, cooked the food, and ran the register. I knew the ins and outs of their lives. I knew the neon lights. I knew the menu backwards, and what was better on Tuesdays. Go get the Greek Islands Special Salad with the signature dressing but start with saganaki cheese. When they light the cheese on fire after smothering it in brandy, the waitress will yell "Opa!" before dousing the flame with a fresh lemon.

Mere words fail to describe not just the love, but the enormity of time spent in GI from working there for years as a teenager to eating there every night we decided not to cook.

What better place to eat immediately after a funeral? Sleepless, haggard, and unable to face opening the refrigerator full of goulash and leftover deli meat, the five of us piled into the Jeep and drove to Greek Islands. We ate slowly, silently, unable to quite tell our friends—behind the counter, at the register, busing the tables—why Michael was not with us, was no longer with us and why he would, in fact, never be with us again. Why he'd never again share the Special Salad or joke and laugh aloud with John (the owner), or smile at Shauna (the hostess), or ask if he could take an extra strawberry-flavored Dum Dum lollipop after paying the check to give to me.

The place was quiet, for we had come after the dinner rush, and the warmth from the people and the kitchen—along with the bright neon lights that lined the ceiling—only served to emphasize the darkness both outside and within.

We sat there prodding at our food in a state of awful quiet.

Then, in a rush of lightning-quick burning grief, tears burst from within Catherine. The force of it was shocking, the kind that makes one choke. Catherine—in the same lavender coat she had worn over the lavender dress at the funeral—quickly caught herself, moisture leaking from her face, all of which was reined in with her left hand that glittered from her wedding ring in the impossibly cheery neon lights.

We all looked at her, and Kent placed his hand gently atop her arm. *We are here Cathy*, the gesture said. We were. She nodded, and placed her hand on top of his own in gratitude. We returned to our food. But no one was hungry.

Our GI family—Eleni the matron waitress consoled her children Paul and Theresa who had deduced what had happened in the distant corner over in section five, Mercury the bus boy, Tikko in the kitchen—glanced over. They all exchanged looks of disbelief. You could see their hearts sinking.

That night, dinner was on the house.

The Grandparental Gunfight

(*At rise: 1367, day. AL sits beneath a blanket. Her insides still not-quite-right after a few days of unexplained discomfort. She is in the downstairs living room curled around a copy of* Harry Potter and the Chamber of Secrets, *trying to finish it as quickly as possible so as to give it to KENT, who is growing increasingly impatient in his wait to read it next. GREY (who has already finished* Chamber of Secrets) *enters from the front door and comes down the stairs, carrying today's mail.*)

GREY: Mail call. This is for you.
AL: For me?
GREY: Why, yes.
AL: What is it?
GREY: It appears to be a letter. In olden times, they were apparently quite popular.

(*They gaze at it, suspicious.*)

AL: Right.
GREY: So it's mail. There is no return address.
AL: (*looking at the letter*) I regret to inform you that it appears to be from my grandparents.

GREY: Really? Huh. I don't smell sulfur. How can you tell?

AL: I can sense their presence with a dowsing rod.

GREY: *(epic eye roll)* I don't believe you.

AL: Well, what can I tell you? I'm not Katie Couric. I don't have any journalistic, magician-level integrity here. I'm a teenager.

GREY: You're also currently a college dropout.

AL: Come to think of it, so are you, so why are you giving me shit?

(GREY *considers this a moment and moves on.*)

GREY: Anyway, I just think it is interesting that you knew it was from them before you even knew there was a letter. (*Feeling it*) My God, it weighs a ton.

AL: Hm. (*Feeling it*) Maybe it is laden with guilt for me to bear for all time!

GREY: Please, just open it.

AL: Sure, happy to. But I feel obligated to warn you: opening this letter would redirect valuable energy from my efforts to not kill my grandparents.

GREY: Al, it is genuinely my job to force you to do things.

AL: It is?

GREY: Yes. I mean, without me opening all of your mail, how would you know about all those trees planted in your Dad's name in Israel?

AL: I wouldn't.

GREY: But truly: I can barely justify my presence in your house as it is. I've been living in the guest room for over a month, we've all dropped out of school, and I'm pretty sure my parents think I've joined a cult.

AL: This is a kind of cult.

GREY: It is. (*Serious voice now*) But I mean it. Al, I'm not just here to distract and entertain and shoo away both the blues and Jehovah's Witnesses. If I'm not here to help you face the hard things . . . then I'm just a college dropout living in your guest room. If I'm not holding your hand while it is hard—if you don't allow me to hold your hand while it is hard—then I—I can't . . .

(GREY is uncharacteristically overcome—the raw emotion on his face is pure exposure, a badge that has let slip the kernel of his inner truth: the truth that GREY is the most sensitive and tender of them all—that GREY is more lost and misdirected and disillusioned than even AL or CATHERINE. They are all holding on to sanity by a thread.

AL looks at GREY and nods "OK." SHE opens the letter and reads it. As SHE pores over the pages, the room fills with soft, overcast, Michigan light, AL folds the pages, calmly places them back into the envelope and glances at GREY.)

  GREY: What is it?
  AL: We've been . . . disowned.

(GREY stares—disbelief slapped across his face.)

  GREY: What does that mean?
  AL: I don't really know. It says that financially and emotionally they
      want nothing more to do with us. Well, with me.

(In a very peculiar way, this knowledge is a kind of relief.)

  AL: *(continued)*. I suppose it means we are truly on our own.
  GREY. Can't you fight them?
  AL. Fight them? How? In a cage match? I honestly wouldn't know how.
      Anyway I hear Albert is a fear-biter.

(GREY looks down at his hands. HE does not know what to say or do.)

  GREY. I'm . . . I'm so, so sorry Al.
  AL: Well what can I say, Grey? You can't bring a knife to a gunfight.

(AL rises with the letter in hand. It occurs to her that words have repercussions. Lesson learned.)

AL: Well. If my absence doesn't affect them, then my presence never
did either. And vice versa, I suppose. Oh, the pride I might've given
them. If only their love hadn't been so conditional.

*(Little did THE SILBERS know: AL did not want their money, SHE
wanted unconditional love. SHE wanted trust and respect and family.
SHE wanted it less for herself, but for her father.)*

AL: Sometimes, our greatest accomplishment is just keeping our mouth
shut.
I didn't do that. I spoke up. I said no. And I am not sorry. *(She
exhales.)* It's OK. Sometimes you win, sometimes you learn.

GREY: Alsy, please—
AL: No, Grey. They demanded my expulsion. They got it.

*(AL makes her way to the bedroom at the top of the stairs. In the days
and years to come, she will not let those who abandoned her stop her
from being generous, from having hope. She enters and closes the door
quietly behind her.)*

The Obligatory Autumn-to-Winter Montage

"What is this? Isolation therapy?"
—*What About Bob?*

The hideous death-beige carpet had been ripped up from the entire upstairs level, the hardwood floors revealed. The new sleigh bed had replaced the Bed of Death, and it felt as though 1367 beckoned us to brighten it in the wake of all that had transpired.

We pushed all the furniture to the middle of each room on the upstairs level, covered the piles in tarps, and drove to Home Depot to pick out bright paints to adorn the top floor of the house with color and life. Dad's old office was revamped into a theatrical guest room; we moved the vintage dark-wood desk all the way downstairs to the lowest level, replacing the table the computer awkwardly sat upon, and we painted it a deep royal purple to go with the copper crown molding. In my room, we took out my childhood desk and bookshelves, pared down my toy selection, and updated the formerly white walls to the adult "Rosalind Blue," with a darker blue trim for the windows. The new master bedroom was, appropriately, the greatest transformation of all—three out of four walls covered in a peaceful, pastel sage green, while the central wall took on an elegant lavender.

It only took us a few days to finish all three rooms. With the complete works of Simon and Garfunkel blazing on a CD player blaring from the hallway, Mom, Kent, and I donned smocks and took up our rollers. We painted and harmonized well into the wee hours of the morning, and, to

this day, I cannot hear "The Sound of Silence" without keeping my nose
alive for the smell of paint.

Of course, eventually, everyone had to go back.

Grey, Kent, and Lilly decided to leave in waves—the theory being that
Mom and I should not be left in the House of Death alone together just
yet.

Lilly departed first. She was the only one of us who hadn't dropped out
of school, and so she had to return to classes and lessons and important
grownup-to-be responsibilities. We understood, of course, but this new
House of Death Family didn't feel complete without her. She promised to
return every few weeks, and she kept her word, driving the 144 miles up
I-75 in that pale blue Dodge caravan over and over again all winter long.

Grey—who had made up his mind to quit school three weeks into the
semester at Cincinnati—needed to withdraw officially, and, a few days
after Lilly left, he went back to campus to wrap up his affairs and pack
his belongings. He then reported back to 1367 in an attempt to regroup,
returning to his home in Wisconsin for the major holidays before reporting back to us for New Year.

Kent stuck around, tending to Mom and me while the others were
away. He received the flowers, organized the sympathy cards, arranged
for people to come over and talk awkwardly in the living room, screened
angry phone calls from the Silbers, and made sure everybody ate. He
wanted to know we would be alright alone in our new silence before
they could return. He headed back to the dairy farm in New Hampshire
to give his two weeks' notice, bid farewell to the goats (and presumably,
Clibbs and Roderigo), and made his way back to Michigan as soon as
he could. His "gap-year off for life experience" tending to goats at the
dairy farm would now be traded for a gap-year of life experience tending to the Silber women in Detroit. Experiencing the realities of second-
hand-grief.

"I'll write," he promised, looking deep into me at the Detroit Wayne County Airport. He held my face in his hands, his long fingers caressing my cheeks tenderly, though his face remained stern. His eyes, usually an icy blue, looked warm now, and one could almost detect the evidence of the thaw along the rims of his lashes. (His stern New England upbringing prevented him from liquefying completely).

"I'll write back," I replied, kissing him.

He walked away, shoulders heavy, farm jacket on his back, hunter green satchel slung casually over his shoulder. Just before entering the brand-new, still foreign, eight-weeks-after-September-11-security-procedures gate, he stopped. He turned back, but he did not return for me—for one last word, look or kiss. Instead, he locked eyes with and then embraced my mother. They held one another there for a long time. I watched, mystified. To this day, neither has ever spoken about what they shared the morning Michael died. This embrace made clear that they had shared something sacred and terrible that only they would ever know. He turned his head, whispered something inaudibly into her ear, then quickly broke away. He kissed me again and ran to the gate, disappearing behind the security barricades and leaving Mom and me alone for the first time in this new part of our new lives.

We stood there numbly, not knowing exactly what to do next.

"What did he whisper to you?" I asked.

"He said '*I love you*.'" She said it matter-of-factly, but the tension in her throat as she swallowed gave away how much it meant.

Then she led the way back to the car that would return us to our first night alone in 1367.

❨ ❩

The next few weeks leading up to Thanksgiving were a blur of readjustments as mom and I stared down the barrel of "the rest of our lives," now without Kent and Grey (and sometimes Lilly) to ease the sorrow. But Kent stayed true to his promise to write and I lived for his letters.

Follansbee Dairy Farm

Sutton, New Hampshire

November 7, 2001

My Own,

I've just told Mrs. F that I won't be staying on past
Thanksgiving. Their farm hand Anders laid it out pretty straight
to me; on finding out that you were in Detroit, he said (in his
broad, New Hampshire accent), "Then what the hell ah you doing
he-ah?" We had a great conversation, really. If he would only take
his own good advice, Anders would be a lot better off.

Now we have something to look forward to. I found a calendar
laying around which I now use to count down the days until I will
see you next. Before the month is out, we'll be together again.

I've actually had a little bit more time the past four days. Time
enough to take a bath at least, which is nice. And to do more
reading. The days are so short that I've been getting off earlier.
Also there's less to do in the winter, which is one reason why I
don't feel so bad leaving. I certainly got the farm experience, and
it did do some good. You just have to help me stay motivated,
none of this waking at 11:00 every day stuff. There's always more
to read if I run out of things to do. And between reading, house
fixing, exercise, love-making, "scene study at home," I'm sure the
time will be filled.

Now comes the waiting. The days can't possibly be short
enough. But I'll see you in my dreams.

                              Always,

                              Kent

To distract me from a migraine, Mom ran a bath and read me the entire copy on a package of Epsom salts with total sincerity in a quiet, soothing voice.

"So as you can see, Al, not only is this bag suitable for migraines, constipation, and fertilizer, but if you have any questions about what I've just read to you, all you have to do is call 1-800-777-3415 in what looks like Indianapolis, and they can answer your questions between 8 a.m. and 8 p.m. eastern standard time. . ."

In those days, we would talk in the bath a lot. I'd sit there covered in bubbles, and we'd chat. (It might sound odd, but it wasn't. It felt bohemian and luxurious, like we were in Hollywood.)

"How was it?" Mom asked one day when I alluded to the fact that Kent and I had, at long last, slept together. (The months preceding the act had been arduous. But the act was laden with the darkness that surrounded us, and not a reflection of our love for one another . . .)

"Good." I said shyly.

She nodded but did not look at me. I glanced at her sideways, catching her face in an expression of concern that we'd never talked about sex until this very moment.

The only time either of my parents had ever broached the subject was when Dad drove me to Chicago to pick up Jeremey after Christmas two years earlier. He had brought it up gingerly, but then spoke of sex with great enthusiasm, not at all shy or squeamish or ashamed to be discussing it so openly with his sixteen-year-old daughter.

"Hey, remember that massage someone gave you for Christmas a few weeks back?" he had said.

"Yeah," I said slowly, uncertain of the terrifying direction in which this line of questioning was leading.

"Well," Dad said with a smile, "that was the second best feeling in the world!"

Horror-struck (as well as suddenly and inexplicably overcome with a priggish, puritanical sense of utter indecency in addition to being *completely mortified* by his nonchalance), I alternated between covering my face and ears while I begged him to stop. My entreaties only resulted in the sound of my father's uncontrollable, rolling laughter.

"Come on, Al!" he said, his voice a pure cheer. "Lighten up! Trust me—the best is yet to come!"

"Dad!" I howled. *"Please stop or I will die."*

Dad pressed a button that promptly auto-locked all the doors to the car. "No way!" His voice rang out again in a tone of such enjoyment I could have sworn he was recording the entire proceeding. "I like to shove my boots in, get my hands in the mud and get *involved!*"

I weathered it as best I could.

I did not want to grow up. Not because I just didn't want to, but because it was yet another way I might burden my already burdened parents. I didn't know I felt that way at the time, but I know it now.

This not-growing-up feeling was baked into my family life. For example, we never discussed the fact that Santa Claus was not real. Mom and I still spoke about Santa as if he were coming to dinner like Elijah (or, say, an actual house guest). It was just a sort of blasé thing: Santa will be coming, naturally. We sort of knowingly talked around the subject during my teens, but we still never really discussed it. Part of me liked that. We were a magical family—and if we weren't going to talk about Santa, then I certainly wasn't going to talk to my parents about sex.

Or about my period, which came at the age of twelve. I hid all evidence of it from my parents for a year with the kind of frantic desperation of an ancient Bedouin girl who doesn't want to be married off to a neighboring tribe the moment she is fertile.

I did not want to grow up. And if I had no choice in the matter, than I certainly was not going to do it with their help.

The Jehovah's Witness

"Gone? You think he's gone?! That's the whole point! He's never gone!"
— *What About Bob?*

(*At rise: AL is at home sometime during Month One of the Aftermath. The doorbell rings. It is getting colder as October churns onward; leaves are falling, and nights are drawing in. Alone, in pajamas and glasses that AL cannot remember changing in or out of. She answers it and her stomach flinches. This is not happening. Oh, but it is.*)

AL: Hi.
JEHOVAH'S WITNESS: Good morning!
AL: (*under her breath*) Not really . . .
JW: Have you heard of Jesus Christ?
AL: . . . I've . . . read his book.
JW: (*Looking AL up and down, assessing her age; He is confused.*) Wait. Why aren't you in school?
AL: My dad is dead.
JW: (*unfazed*) But you are a teenager.
AL: In college.
JW: Then why aren't you in college?
AL: I'm taking some time off.
JW: Why?
AL: Because my dad is dead.

(AL wants to say, "No, Sir, I'm at home because I just hate responsibility that much," but she doesn't. She awkward-pauses with this man and lets it stew.)

> **JW:** Would you like to see your father again?
> **AL:** Is this a joke?
> **JW:** No! *(Joyfully)* You can see your father again if you give your soul
> over to Jesus Christ! Here, see the drawing in this pamphlet?

(Pause. AL inspects the pamphlet. It is the kind of drawing you see in cheap children's magazines at the pediatrician's office—children running towards the elderly in a perfect, sunny, Dr. Seuss-like field of heavenly bliss.)

> **AL:** Um, you need to go.
> **JW:** May I come in?

(AL shrugs her shoulders.)

> **AL:** You know what? Sure.

(The JW does the whole speech. He stands up, acts stuff out. He is impassioned and expressive and sort of beautiful without being the kind of desperate one might expect. But AL just sits there in her week-old clothes, numb, no will of her own to stop it. Finally, it ends.)

> **JW:** So, do you have any questions?
> **AL:** Yes. *(For a second, she considers asking him if he would like to
> hear a knock knock joke, but thinks better of it. These are not
> the people you start knock knock jokes with.)* Does it feel good?
> **JW:** *(taken aback)* I'm sorry?
> **AL:** To have done the whole speech?
> **JW:** What do you mean?

AL: You must not ever be able to get the whole thing out; so many people slam doors in your faces. I mean you are . . . well, you are like the original telemarketers. Does it feel good to have done the whole thing?

(*JW stares at AL. There is a part of him that sees he cannot hide from her—a young person so raw they are incapable of judgment either passed or received, and he looks, for an instant, uneasy. But this quickly fades as he sees the humor and truth in her question. This man is a Jehovah's Witness, but he is also her neighbor, and there is a part of him that is so gentle and well meaning it breaks her heart. The JW smiles and all his theatricality wanes.*)

JW: It does, you know.
AL: What?
JW: Feel good.
AL: Good.
JW: Thank you.
AL: Thank you.

(*They smile at one another.*)

AL: But now you probably should go.
JW: OK.

(*He'll be fine. He will always have his friends at the Kingdom Hall.*)

Another Letter from Kent

Follansbee Dairy Farm
Sutton, New Hampshire

November 10, 2001

Dearest Love,

I've finally just received your first letter since our parting.
That may be the only negative thing about my coming to you; no
long distance loving. As usual, your letter melted me. All your
wonderful cadences are tantalizingly hinted at when you write.
It's wonderful. And I love that little drawing of course. It seems
strange to me how sure I am that I could spend the rest of my
life with you. But it's true, isn't it. We've already spent a month
living together, and I have no worries about the time to come, only
excitement and anticipation.

    I've thought about next year, the school decision. Previously
I refused to factor you into the equation, thinking it would bias
the decision. But I've come to realize that not only do I want to be
with you, but I won't live without you. I don't know how it will pan
out practically, but I don't see how we could function so far apart.

Think of our possible just-us life: we'd have all our books, our own bed. And if we went to the same school, we'd get to work together again. That'd be very nice.

Perhaps I'm getting a bit premature. But you should know that I think about our life together. We do seem to inspire one another. I hope, even though it seems fantastical at times that we can be close next year. I don't think I could handle the distance very well. And there's really no call for it, so why go through all the trouble?

I'm looking forward to my trip west. I'm going home to pick up my stuff, then my dad and I are driving to Cincinnati. It has the potential to be a very healthy time for us. I always feel like we both try so hard to connect, but we keep missing the mark. I want to tell him about you, about us, about how we are together. I realized just a few days ago that if my father were to die now, I would be left with an unbearable regret. And now is the time to make things right with him. I'm confident that it will happen.

I'm getting to be quite a handy man here on the farm. Let's see, I fixed the Volvo muffler, the rear lights, installed new windows in the store room, fixed some leaky pipes, built some sheep feeders (I'm quite proud of those), installed some equipment in the greenhouse—the list just goes on! All this problem solving is really quite fun. And useful information for, say, a husband to have.

I can't wait for all the wonderful things we'll fill our days with when we're together again. I just love going to the theater. The opera, of course. You're such a stimulating person to experience life with; a great date. I definitely want to commence our Shakespeare reading. Perhaps Henry IV; you know I prefer the histories.

Well, my love, I'll say goodnight once more. Fortunately, I can look forward to sweet dreams of you.

Always Yours,

Kent

So, the Story about
My Parents Goes Like This . . .

During the summer of 1976, my parents met on an airplane in Spain. It was the summer of the Montreal Olympics and of the American Bicentennial, and in one of those classic (almost unbelievable) love stories, both my parents were on individual trips to Europe to heal themselves— Cathy from a not-quite-right young marriage, Michael from a painful divorce involving a very young son, as well as a generally existential mid-life moment.

Twenty-seven-year-old Cathy's parents were living in Barcelona, and her summer spent with them was more than merely an opportunity to earn graduate credits; it served as a simultaneous escape from her painfully ill-fated marriage to Dennis.

Ah, Dennis. Now, I have never met Dennis, but he exists in my life as a legend, the same as those stories about Walt Disney being cryogenically frozen or the existence of the Yeti. While undergrads at California Polytechnic University (AKA Cal Poly) in the late 1960s, Dennis and Cathy had been introduced by a mutual friend named Kay Jacobs. Dennis was a basketball star and Cathy's first real love. They courted, dated, fell in love, fell out, broke up, and fell back in—all of which culminated in Cathy concluding, "If it hurts this much it must be love." This ultimately led to their marriage. It was a romance of operatic overtures. My mom once told me that he was the first man she ever slept with, and, with her upbringing, she thought she had to marry him.

Shortly after their marriage, a calamitous injury befell Dennis, preventing him from ever playing basketball again. Dennis limped all six foot eight inches of himself into the popular "nouveau Eastern thought" movement of the era, and he lit incense, began meditating, and practicing free love. He took a vow of celibacy that seemed to be applicable only to his wife. It wasn't the ideal set-up for a new marriage.

Dennis insisted that the problems in their marriage were hers. Cathy was "unenlightened," he said. She was "cramping his style." And, from Cathy's perspective, she didn't mean to be uncooperative—it's just that she kept coming home to a house full of incense to find Dennis naked in bed feeding fruit to their neighbors. It was somewhat awkward.

Cathy tried to chant, to dissolve her ego, to meditate, to "get on board" in the lotus position—all to no avail. No matter how hard she tried, she couldn't do it—it was not who she was, and this new, experimental Dennis was simply not the man she had married.

"Do you even love me?" Cathy would ask.

"I'm still here, aren't I?" Dennis would reply.

Then, in the summer of 1976, Cathy found Dennis in bed with Kay Jacobs. That was it. Cathy left and joined Delalberto and Florence (after Cathy left her biological mother's custody, she always referred to Florence as her *mother*, and to them collectively as her *parents*) in Barcelona.

When late August arrived—and, with it, the end of her visit—Cathy's parents drove her to the airport. They had not discussed her turmoil once the entire summer. She burst into tears in her mother's arms. She wept while Florence held her and dried her tears. Then she told Cathy, "You will never leave him unless you truly believe you can love someone else."

They would turn out to be prophetic words.

Meanwhile, Michael was on vacation in Europe. His workmates had insisted upon it. Michael never really wanted to be a lawyer, but he was a hero to his colleagues, and a nasty divorce from a first wife he later admitted he'd married out of sheer "I'm-thirty-one-and-not-married" panic combined with a painfully difficult situation with their very young son had all taken its toll. His coworkers at the law office had insisted he "get out of town." So he had.

He had gone to Barcelona and then his intended journey on to Paris was foiled when, for no other reason than perpetually unreliable trains, the train to Paris had been cancelled. So he decided to cut his losses in Barcelona and head home early.

But he was late for his flight. Searching for the gate, he put his bags down on the ground to get his bearings—and it was then that he saw it: two women, a mother comforting a daughter in tears. *Beautiful . . .* he thought before the final boarding for the flight was called and he promptly flew to the gate.

Incredible, yes? But they did not meet there.

They met on the airplane after the flight from Barcelona landed in Madrid.

Michael (a man who *always* got up to disembark before the plane even touched the ground) passed Catherine (the woman who *always* waited until everyone was off the plane) and stopped dead. It was the beautiful, tearful woman from the airport. He spluttered, his tongue turned to lead. Unable to speak, he feebly "after-you" hand gestured to the beautiful woman, who was even more beautiful than he had realized from afar.

"No, thank you," she said. "I'm just going to stay here until everyone is off the plane."

He stood still, staring at the beautiful woman who was reading a book to pass the time, a sea of angry Europeans screaming behind him. Still unable to speak, he did the gesture again.

Cathy, starring at the impossibly gorgeous, European-looking man repeated, "No, thank you," she said slowly again, raising her voice as if that would help. "*I am going to stay here until everyone is off the plane.*"

"Oh," he spluttered. "I'm really sorry to have spoiled your plans . . . "

Michael couldn't believe the lameness of his response, but Catherine found this man so earnest, so charming, and his response so delightfully sweet that she burst out laughing and she did indeed get off the plane.

They never could have guessed that they were both headed to San Francisco, where they lived just a few miles apart. They never could have imagined that they would spend the remainder of that twenty-hour journey westward seated beside one another, slowly falling in love in the airports, on the planes, both speaking their innermost truths for the first time in their lives. But that's exactly what happened.

Just before the plane landed, Michael got nervous.

"Look, Cathy. I can't believe I am saying this but I . . . am in love with you. And I would never want to be responsible for a marriage breaking apart," he said. "But here is my business card. If I don't hear from you in six months, call just to tell me how you are doing."

Cathy burst into tears as Michael distanced himself from this beguiling, miserably married woman, and, in an act of restraint and honor, changed seats for the last hour of the journey, so profoundly in love with her was he.

When they got off the plane, they went their separate ways. But Catherine already knew she would see him again. Her mother's words rang out to her like a prophecy.

At the airport, Cathy was greeted by Dennis and Kay Jacobs, who told her they were leaving the next morning to meditate in the desert for eight weeks.

"Fine," Catherine conceded, because, finally, it was.

Cathy returned home, and Dennis and Kay did indeed leave the following morning. In the wake of their departure, Cathy looked over the brand new condo on the cliffs of Santa Cruz that she had shared with her brand new husband, then went to her wallet, and took out Michael Silber's business card.

It was ten o'clock in the morning. She picked up the phone and dialed the number. As it was ringing she panicked, thinking, *What if he doesn't remember me?* But before she could hesitate, he answered the phone.

"*Buenos días,*" she said, her voice shaking but sure. "Are you still in love?"

"Oh," he sighed. "You bet."

She drove her red vintage 240Z to Michael's office in her best outfit, she was buzzed in by the secretary, and entered the office.

There was kissing. There were fireworks.

That weekend was a flurry of love, Northern California activities, and introductions to every single person Michael knew. When the weekend was over, he turned to her and asked, "So are you moving in? Are we getting married or what?"

He smiled. He was absolutely sincere. So she trusted him.

And that was that. The rest is history.

You know, whenever I tell that story, people are speechless. They don't believe it. They say it sounds like a movie script. But it is real. It happened. These things do. Happen.

Years ago, on the twentieth anniversary of that fateful plane journey, the three of us went out to dinner and I first heard the "airplane story"— told with all the fully explored emotions, the little details, the kiss they shared. I don't think I'll ever forget the looks on their faces as they told me the story and relived the memories.

"Her voice was. . . like a bell," my father said. "I just couldn't stop listening to her, and to every single thing she had to say."

Mom blushed, smiling at him.

It would take me many years to truly understand the nature of what my mother lost.

Big Trash Day

It was the night before "big trash" day—the day you put out your larger items on the curb for it to be carted away to the undiscovered country.

Last month's initial purge had been like grief Viagra—we were on a roll. Redoing the house, beginning with the upstairs, had become the largest chunk of our daily activities.

Some of it was marvelous. The strong scent of paint filled the house, its acidic odor burning off the smells of disease, and the windows flew open, washing the place clean with the freshness and oncoming frosts of November in the air.

But other parts were not marvelous at all.

This night, I sat at the curb, my body unfathomably fatigued; it was all I could do to remain awake. My back and every muscle were sore, my head dense with dulling fog, even my breasts were tender and aching. The steady rain upon the street, rooftops, and curb fell upon me too as I sat in a ball in the seat of my father's black leather swivel chair—the noisy, worn out chair that had lived in his office. It was the one my mother had always hated, the one I associated with the sound of his IBM typewriter, that still smelled of him and held the unmistakable imprint of his body. I sat, feeling that imprint left upon the worn leather, soaked to the bone in the freezing rain. I would stay there all night.

The memories began to flash.

I am thirteen and sitting on the bed with Dad, frustrated beyond all reason by my homework for Eighth Grade Money Management class. I do not understand money or how to manage it, and, despite my sulky attitude, he is very slowly explaining everything with great patience until I absolutely do. Only a few years back, we sat in the very same positions reading the Chronicles of Narnia, and now I am being asked to manage money like an adult and I do not want to grow up. But most of all I do not want to disappoint him.

It is Thanksgiving 1998 and it feels as though everyone in town (and several friends from out of town), are at 1367 gathered around our piano singing show tunes—duets and solos, until finally we all erupt in an emotional chorus of the Act 1 finale of *Ragtime*, my father's eyes closed, his voice the strongest and most impassioned of us all.

I am fourteen and driving to Groves High School with Dad, just as we have driven to every school, every single morning, since time began. He pulls up right in front of the back entrance on Evergreen Road. We hug, I kiss him on the cheek, and we exchange "I love yous" before I grab my purple backpack and run inside. Before heading inside I catch the eye of Sarah Radke, a girl two classes ahead of me whom I've known since the summer before we moved to Michigan. She's getting out of the car driven by her father, whom I smile and wave to. Mr. Radke's face looks thoughtful as I make my way inside. I will learn a few years later how much watching the Silbers say goodbye at the school entrance means to him. I'll come to learn that when he's having particular trouble with Sarah, that he will say, "You know how Al and Michael Silber say goodbye to one another every morning? If you could ever do that for me—just once—it would mean the world to me." I will learn, years later (when Mr. Radke also dies prematurely, in his case from pancreatic cancer), that Sarah will listen. It will, in its own small way, change a little piece of their relationship.

It is the third Saturday of August, 1995—the weekend of the Woodward Dream Cruise, a classic car event held annually in Detroit to celebrate the essence of Motor City. After World War II, people began to "cruise" in their cars along Woodward, from drive-in to drive-in, often looking for friends who were also out for a drive, celebrating a new sense of freedom. Now the Woodward Dream Cruise is the world's largest one-day automotive event, drawing 1.5 million people and 40,000 classic cars each year from around the entire world. We've lived here a year, and we decide to pull up to Woodward and take a peek at the event that spans all the way from Pontiac to the State Fair Grounds inside the Detroit City limits, just south of Eight Mile Road. It is absolutely majestic. Most of the cars on display are vintage models from the 1950s to the early 1970s—muscle cars, hot rods, T-birds and Corvettes, but there are some turn-of-the-century gems, some custom, collector and special interest vehicles all dating across the last century and change.

I am in the kitchen, and it's one of the rare nights when Dad has taken it upon himself to "cook" dinner. Mom and I stare down at our plates; they contain masses of once-colorful vegetables, slopped in butter, with skins charred so black that the food is indistinguishable from *food*. So close are these once-vegetables to barbeque coal one might as well be eating coal straight from the bag. "Don't panic," Dad urges. "It's not burnt. It's *Cajun*."

I am playing Miss Hannigan in the third grade production of *Annie* at El Rodeo School in Beverly Hills, California. It is my first theatrical experience and, even though I am merely eight, I know that I am a hoot as I copy Carol Burnett's performance from the film, down to every intonation and drunken idiosyncrasy. It is the morning of the day of the performance, and I am not the least bit nervous. At breakfast Dad says, "You should eat." But I do not. And then, hungry and tired by evening, I forget the words to my song for the first time ever while singing my big number. (Since then, I have always eaten something before a performance).

I am on the banks of Quarton Lake getting ready for my very first ice-skating sojourn outdoors on a natural body of water. We have lived in Birmingham, Michigan for just a few weeks and Quarton Elementary School (where I have recently been enrolled in the fourth grade) has an annual Quarton Lake Skate that features skating for parents and kids alike, as well as a vat of hot cocoa. I hold my dad's hand as I take my first-ever steps, skating until my nose is red from the exertion and cold.

I am at Dairy Deluxe on Woodward and Fourteen Mile. It's the classic Birmingham summer hangout that goes by many unofficial titles (among them: the Twirly Dip, Double D, and DD). The joy of a visit to Dairy Deluxe is indeed in the quality of the ice cream and various confections, as well as the little quirks that make it (and have kept it) so small-town charming over the years. In reality, Dairy Deluxe is really nothing more than a hut with a giant, neon ice cream cone sign atop it. But, to me, it is much, much more. The same people have been running Dairy Deluxe for well over twenty years, and they still write down your order by hand on bits of paper, dole change out without calculating it first on a register, and make your order themselves, handing it to you through a teeny tiny window.

I am driving along Maple Road, rounding the strange curve any nonnative Birminghamer would find confusing—right at the twisty point where suddenly you are confronted with what I always blasphemously referred to as "Christian Corner," where the "First" Methodist, Presbyterian, and Lutheran churches all appear in a clump, sprung up like eager flowers drenched in holy water. On the same strip of Maple sits the beloved Mills Pharmacy, where Dad used to take me in to buy as much candy as possible for a single dollar. (It was his way of teaching me about counting out and budgeting money.) Individually wrapped Swedish Fish and Sour Patch Kids are only ten cents and candy bars fifty cents. There are Laffy Taffy, Pixy Stix, Runts, Nerds, Necco Wafers—the list is endless. A charming bearded man behind the old-fashioned candy counter used to greet us, and he was so like the one in *Willy Wonka and the Chocolate Factory* that I practically expected him to burst into song at any moment. It was pure magic.

I am on the curb in the chair on big trash day. I have been out here for hours. I am soaking wet. I realize that every memory is now merely another painful nostalgic touchstone. None of it, not one single thing, will ever be magical again.

I am touched on the shoulder by Lilly. The moment had arrived to just surrender. I am brought inside, shaking and miserable.

I am lost without him.

PART FOUR:
THE AFTER-AFTERMATH

"I Wish" / "I Know"

In sixth grade, when asked by our middle school music teacher to bring in a recording of our favorite music, everyone else brought in Ace of Base, Boyz II Men, and Mariah Carey. I? I brought in the 1989 Original Cast Recording of *Into the Woods*. That's right. I brought in Stephen Sondheim. Even at eleven, I could appreciate a 6/9 time signature, internal rhyming, all things Robert Westenberg, and poignant social parallels.

Into the Woods—with music and lyrics by Stephen Sondheim and a book by James Lapine—is a masterpiece of the musical theater about the inner lives and backstories of the world's most famous (and infamous) fairy-tale characters. We are fortunate as a culture to have the original production preserved not only on audio recording, but in a beautifully filmed live video of the stage performance. I grew up devouring both.

A narrator guides us through the first act of familiar stories: Cinderella and her Prince, Jack and his beanstalk, Rapunzel, Little Red Riding Hood, and some new characters such as a Witch, a childless Baker and his Wife, all crisscrossing and influencing one another in ways our children's stories were never privy to.

The curtain rises, and the audience is welcomed by the Narrator,[23] who

---

23   Incidentally, played originally by Tom Aldridge, who also plays Mr. Gutmann in *What About Bob?*, thus, making him a god among men

cheerfully opens with, "Once upon a time" followed by a now-celebrated and utterly identifiable series of chords, and then it's lights up on the characters! The first is Cinderella. She sings a phrase that is to become the haunting theme of the evening: "I wish . . . "

Every one of our characters has a wish—to go to the festival, to have a child, for fortune, wealth, security, beauty. These are the things that they want. And so they wish.

By the end of the first act, every character has achieved their well-known conclusions, actualized their wishes, and we celebrate with them in a rollicking act one finale celebrating happily "Ever After!"

Things get more complicated in the second act.

After intermission we learn Cinderella's prince is unfaithful, and life in the luxurious palace is unfulfilling. The Baker and His Wife have their child, and they are ill content. With the wolf dead, Little Red feigns confidence in the shadow of her attack. The Witch has lost not only her daughter Rapunzel, but her magic powers in exchange for physical beauty. And above all, Jack has murdered the giant in the sky, and angered his wife, who now threatens to destroy their kingdom if she cannot take her revenge on her husband's killer.

Slowly, over the course of the incredibly difficult second act, it is not an exaggeration to say that nearly everyone suffers in the wake of the Giant.

This musical opened on Broadway in 1989, at the very height of the AIDS epidemic, and, as a child born in the middle of the crisis, I suppose I only now realize that the actors in the original production were suffering losses every day—of their friends, family, and members of their communities. Mind-obliterating, countless losses and daily fear—all of it lacking in any kind of reason. A different kind of Giant had ravaged their kingdom.

When I was a child, I suppose I was too young to understand the story with this level of intensity, but, as Little Red Riding Hood so simply explains in act one: "I know things now."

Into the Woods is a piece I have never truly seen myself inside of—somewhat unusual for an actor, as we tend to see where we would, or would like to, fit inside a story. But with *Into the Woods*, I've always been in the audience, seeing the whole picture, never precisely identifying with any individual story arc.

Until now.

In the final few moments of the play, the too-old-to-be-babied and too-young-to-be-ready Little Red Riding Hood sits in shock. She is already vulnerable, traumatized from her experience with the wolf in act one; yet, in this moment she cannot move in the wake of losing her entire family. Her face is strained, but no tears come. She realizes slowly that she is alone in the world—a child with nothing but a wolf-skin coat on her back.

Beside her is Cinderella. She is dressed in rags once more, and, having left the Prince, she is on her own again to face the world as a stronger and smarter woman than before.

Dreams shattered, lives forever altered, the two women sit there. And from the depths of Little Red's soul, comes the musical phrase we know from what seems like forever ago, a cry from her soul so straightforward, so true, yet so painful she can barely utter it: "I wish . . . "

Cinderella looks at her. Not with pity. Cinderella cannot grant her wish. No one can. The kingdom is annihilated. People are dead. Life will never be the same. Her childhood is ended. Cinderella responds simply, "I know."

Four words. Just four. Yet this brief exchange is the summation of my entire life.

Little Red, my eighteen-year-old self, and Cinderella, the self of today. Would that I could look that eighteen-year-old girl straight in the eye, as Cinderella does for Little Red. I wish I could tell her that she is absolutely right—this is the bottom of the well of human pain. That her innocence is shattered, her childhood at its end. *Loss like this will never be "OK," darling girl*, I would say. *It will only grow familiar and thus less harrowing. There may never be anything deeper or more painful to wish away, ever again.*

But now? Now Little Red has earned her passage to the human race. She may now arrive upon humanity's shores as the inextinguishable woman she is destined to become—that *this exact tragedy*, in time, if she allows it, will make her soul the richer and escort her to her highest self.

Those four words capture the essence of both versions of myself, of where I sit today as perpetual eighteen-year-old and ever-evolving adult. As I write these words upon the page, looking back to my own "once upon a time," exactly half my life ago. Before the Giant ravaged *my* kingdom, taking all but my heartbeat.

Barren

"What is 'If you are on fire?'"
"What is 'An attack of the undead.'"
"What is 'If there isn't any open wilderness for miles.'"
"What is 'Public restrooms.'"

It's November 27, 2001. I find myself in my own personal game of *Jeopardy!*. The category is Last Resorts. And just my luck: I've gotten the Daily Double.

I was on a recovery table dressed in Kent's long-sleeved light blue shirt that, to this day, still sits below my nightstand. My thoughts raced—wildly—of what had happened, what was happening, what would become of me in the most immediate moments, and what would happen for years to come.

I had chosen to be alone. We all knew Grey had a proclivity toward being troubled by such matters. We did him and ourselves a favor: we elected not to tell him. Instead, Kent suggested they go out for the day. And I was not about to be that girl who showed up with her mother. Plus, did I really want to trouble my mother further?

I got myself into this, I thought. *I will get myself out.*

Everyone knows that teen sexuality is a landfill of anguish and uncertainties. Anyone who has not dipped a toe into the toxic pool of adolescent sexual experiences is both a weirdo and also one of the four luckiest people on Earth.

Sometimes you are so in love, you think you are going to burst. Sometimes, you are so wracked with need, with unutterable emotion, that you long for any scrap of comfort. Sometimes two young people connect with each other in an unalloyed display of love amidst a hurricane of despair. And sometimes, you do everything right, take every precaution, and everything, still, goes terribly wrong.

My father was dead. I'd dropped out of college and been disowned by my family. But today's event? I had tipped my king.

I got myself into this. I will get myself out.

And so I did what I knew I had to.

"Your body might never be exactly the same," the nurse said a while later, gazing down at my chart.

"OK," I replied, still numb.

"Fine," the nurse said. "Sign here," she instructed, looking me over. *How young,* her eyes said, *what a goddamn shame it is.*

"Besides," I continued. "If I ever wanted to feel good about my body, I should never have become an actress."

"Right," she said, and spun on her heel, taking her leave of the dark, New Age-y room.

On my left was a wan, older woman in the bed next to me. She was groaning softly. I imagined she felt like I did—that she hurt more in her choked mind than in the body that had just been emptied. I leaned over toward her and our eyes locked.

Then she extended her hand.

Her fingers groped for mine, for some kind—any kind—of connection. This woman was all alone too. I let her hold my hand and returned a small squeeze. That was all we could do.

Do you want to ask me what it felt like to become a statistic? The answer: not great. I had done everything right. I had been a good girl. The perfect child who didn't make mistakes.

But I never wavered. Not from this.

At home, Mom put me into the makeshift office bed, brought me a heating pad, and let me rest. A few hours later, Kent and Grey returned from their outing. I made overtures about not feeling well.

And we never spoke of it again.

Controversial-ku

"It reminds me of my favorite poem, which is,
'Roses are red, violets are blue, I'm a schizophrenic. . . and so am I.'"
—Bob Wiley, speaking to patients in a mental hospital, *What About Bob?*

1.
Asleep. Silence shook
me like a soldier, awake.
I've passed through a door.

2.
There are things I can't—
(It shall never be undone.)
—say. But this I can.

A Trip to U of M

A few days after Thanksgiving—the week after my abortion—we decided to see a touring production of *Tartuffe* playing at the University of Michigan in Ann Arbor. Why not, right? What better way to pass the time than with 17th century problems as told in rhyming couplets? After the show, I spied a classmate from high school. I thought I'd be able to dodge him and escape without notice, but we caught eyes and I dutifully approached from across the theater.

"Hi Dave," I said awkwardly.

"Oh, hey Alex," Dave Breen—he of the high school popular crowd—replied with his signature nonchalance. I tried not to wince at his use of Alex. "What are you doing here?"

"I just saw the show."

"Right," he said. "But you don't go to school here, do you?"

"No."

"Right. But you're a freshman right now, right?"

"Sure." I suppose it was technically true, and even if it wasn't, it was the easiest response.

"So are you home for Thanksgiving or something?" This was by far and away, the most concern Dave Breen had ever shown me, unless you counted our on-stage exchanges in the plays at Groves High School.

"Um—" I hesitated. "Well, not exactly."

It started to dawn on Dave Breen that something was fishy. "Oh, I'm sorry," he said. "I didn't mean to pry—"

"My dad died."

The was a pause. A pause during which Dave Breen just stared at me. "Pardon?"

"A few weeks ago," I said.

These few monosyllabic words sputtered out in what felt like a lifetime.

"He's dead. He died."

Dave didn't say a word.

( )

Dave was actually a kid from high school who knew my dad. He starred in the "Playing Frisbee with the Popular Kids" story, which goes like this:

(AL— *a freshman in a large, typical public American high school in the spring of 1998 in a Midwestern "Wonder Years-y" suburb. The phone rings. AL answers it.*)

FRESHMAN AL: Hello, Silber residence.

POPULAR SENIOR: Hey Al, this is Popular Senior calling.

FRESHMAN AL: Oh. Um, hi, Popular Senior. What's going on?

POPULAR SENIOR: Well . . .

POPULAR JUNIOR: (*talking from the background*) Ask him! He said to call! He said he'd play!

POPULAR SENIOR: Sorry, that was Popular Junior Guy.

FRESHMAN AL: I see.

POPULAR SENIOR: Well, we were calling because we were just hanging in the park and wondered if . . .

(AL *holds her breath at the thought the popular guys want to hang out with her.*)

POPULAR SENIOR: (*continued*). . . . if your Dad wanted to play
Frisbee with us.

(*Pause.*)

POPULAR JUNIOR: (*from the background*) So is he coming?
FRESHMAN AL: Let me . . . um . . . get him. One second.
POPULAR SENIOR: Well, we're actually, like, down the street. Can we
just come over?
FRESHMAN AL: Sure. I'll let my dad know.

(*Hangs up. Yells upstairs.*)

FRESHMAN AL: Dad!
DAD: Yeah?
FRESHMAN AL: The Popular Boys wanted to know if you want to play
Frisbee with them. Did you say you'd hang out with them?
DAD: Well . . . Um, yeah. *(AL displays further disbelief)* Can I go?
I promise not to say anything embarrassing. I'll be really cool, I
promise!
FRESHMAN AL: Dad! They are the most popular boys! This is so
ridiculous!
DAD: But, Al, I really want to play Frisbee! Please?
FRESHMAN AL: Oh, God. *Fine.*

(*Doorbell rings. AL answers the door.*)

FRESHMAN AL: Hey.
POPULAR BOYS: Hey. Um, is your dad home?
FRESHMAN AL: Yeah. I'll go get him.

(*AL turns around and sees her dad right beside the door looking really
anxious to go and play with the boys. Like a kid.*)

FRESHMAN AL: Oh, go ahead, Dad. For heaven's sake!
DAD: Thanks, Al! See ya!
POPULAR BOYS: Later, Al.

That was pretty typical. A group of über-cool teenagers thinking my dad was the absolute best. Of course the über-cool teenagers could get in line, because everyone thought Mike Silber was the absolute best.

( )

Back in the auditorium, Dave Breen stood immobile before me.

"Oh my God Alex, I am . . . " He looked at the floor, his hands in fists within his winter coat pockets. "I am really so, so sorry to hear that."

"It's OK," I replied without thinking.

I wanted it to be OK. For him. Despite the fact that we had never really been friends, I wanted him to come out of this conversation unscathed. I imagined I could hear his heart crumbling from an arm's length away.

I reconsidered. "I mean, of course it is not OK," I said. "But . . . Well, anyway, thank you." I could feel the acid rise in my throat.

"I, uh . . . " he hesitated. "I really liked your dad." Dave's eyes were moist, and locked on the bizarrely bright carpet on the floor of the theater. "A lot."

"Take care, Dave."

And I left him there, alone in the emptying theater.

Rabbi Syme

"Dr. Marvin. You can help me. For the first time in my life,
I feel like there's hope. I feel like I can be somebody."
—*What About Bob?*

Two months after the funeral, I went back to see Rabbi Syme.
I'd known Rabbi Syme for approximately two hours, but I was
in need of some kind of guidance—spiritual or otherwise—and I didn't
know where to turn. I walked into Temple Beth El ready to order up a
super-sized platter of spiritual solutions. Despite the brevity of our relationship, I felt inexplicably close to him, compelled beyond logic to spend
time in the company of the sweet, wise man who had, in such a brief
collection of minutes, given me the ultimate gift of the eulogy.

By the time I walked down the hallway and reached the rabbi's office,
at Temple Beth El I realized I'd made a terrible mistake. Not only did
I barely know him, but I knew so little of Judaism and had railed so
harshly against it my whole life because I had only ever associated it with
my horrible grandparents. I thought about fleeing, but I entered and sat
across from him. Two almost-strangers in two chairs.

"So. How are you doing?" he asked.

What was I supposed to say? "Fine, thank you, Rabbi."

I wanted to tell him about everything. About my grandparents and my
family and the disowning. About dropping out of college and my mother
and Kent. About the life-altering decision I'd made the other day. About
that.

"How is your mother?"

What was I supposed to tell him? I thought. *Do I recount the real blood and guts of living together in the house where my father had died? Should I confess that we were holding on by the single fiber of a thread?*

"Better than can be expected," I said.

"You know," he said, "delivering a eulogy gives a person an extraordinary head start when it comes to healing. You should know that, I'm sure you do. But I hope you are being patient."

"I'm doing my best," I replied. I hoped I was.

"And your family?"

Well, well, well, Rabbi Syme. This is all getting a bit personal! I usually wait until the third date to list my favorite Mandy Patinkin roles in order of sexiness, intensity and beard length, let alone discuss my batshit bonkers family. But I suppose I can make an exception here. Although, how does one explain one's grandparents when "that one time Edna kidnapped me" is only the sixth most dysfunctional story on a very long list?

But I didn't say that. Instead, I just said, "I don't really know."

Rabbi Syme nodded. "I sensed as much. They were . . . unusual."

Rabbi Syme's Spidey skills for the win.

We talked for a long while that day, Rabbi Syme and I. Rabbi Syme was more than just my first spiritual advisor. He was the first adult who was more interested in my cultivation of wisdom than of knowledge. Knowledge is information—a collection of facts. Wisdom is the poetry inside those facts. Wisdom relies on more than mere description. It is the difference between a photograph that captures exactly what something looked like in the moment and a photograph that captures exactly the way it *felt*. Memory through a lens.

"Do you know the *Shema' Koleinu*," Rabbi Syme asked.

"Rabbi, I wasn't invited to many Bar Mitzvahs. I'm kind of a Cashew."

He stared at me blankly.

"A Catholic-Jew," I explained. "An interfaith secularization situation."

"Ah," he said.

"But I was invited to both the Steinman kids' parties and, for what it's worth, I played Golde in *Fiddler* sophomore year of high school—"

He put up a hand to stop me, kind but swift. "I understand. Let me explain. The *Shema' Koleinu* is the sixteenth paragraph of a central prayer of Judaism called the *Amidah*, which is the core of every Jewish worship service. It reads:

סִימְחַרְב לְבַּקְנ ,וְנִילְעַ סְחַרְן סוּחַ ,וּנִיהְלֶא 'ה ,וּנֵלוֹק עַמְשׁ ,נָמְחַרְה בָּא וּנְכְלַמ רָיְנָפְּלְמו ,הָתָא סִינוּנְחַתוֹ תוּלְפְּת עַמוֹשׁ לֹא יִכ ,וּנְתָלְפְּת' תֶא וְֹצַרְבו .וּנֵבִישְׁת לֹא םְקִיַר.

It is translated as 'Hear our voice, O Lord our God; spare us and have mercy upon us, and accept our prayer in mercy and favor.'[24] 'Hear our voice' is the essence of this prayer—and I sense that your voice has always been heard, both of the spoken and the sung variety. The eulogy proves that."

I nodded, not entirely understanding where he was leading me. All I knew was that I was willing to follow.

"What do you think of the passage?"

No one had ever asked me anything remotely like this. I grew hot and uneasy, fearing I would offend him or say the wrong thing.

"I really don't know how to respond."

"There is no right or wrong here, Alexandra," the Rabbi said. "It's just a simple question. One of the beauties of Judaism is this ancient tradition of the dialogic process. Jews recognizing that understanding comes from meaningful exchanges and from challenges—not only with one another but with God Himself."

A light bulb went on. "Oh! Like in *Fiddler* how Tevye has a kind of dialogue with God!"

"Exactly like that. God and Tevye have a very personal relationship."

"I really like that."

---

24   Translation from *The Standard Prayer Book* by Simeon Singer (1915), public domain

"So do I," he said with a smile. "So? What do you think of the call to 'hear our voice?'"

"We all . . . want to be heard."

"Yes."

"And we all struggle to listen?"

"I think so." He leaned in. "'Hear our voice' is a very simple request that shows we want to engage beyond ourselves. It acknowledges the desire to be heard, and it validates that desire. And that's why you are here today, isn't it? To be heard?"

It certainly was. I nodded wordlessly.

He continued. "The prayer goes on: 'Renew our days, as of old.' It's almost as if the speaker is a little skeptical. Alexandra, do you think it is possible to recover the days of the past?"

"No, but . . . " I hesitated. And then I saw.

My father was dead. That was the fact. But if I could turn these days of pain into lessons, that awful fact could become poetry that would continue for the rest of my life. Yes, the past is "passed"— it is unrecoverable and none of us can live there. But the wisdom gained by reflection upon that past is why we are alive. To make meaning. To understand better. I got it. If prayers were *only* knowledge, prayers would fail.

I looked at Rabbi Syme.

"Do you believe, Alexandra?" he asked.

"I believe *you*." I did—it wasn't an evasion.

"You know what I'm asking."

"I do. I can't believe I'm saying it but I do. I believe in something."

"Well, good. 'Something' is possibility. 'Something' is something."

I thanked Rabbi Syme and left. I would not see him again for seventeen years. But his impact would be with me, his name forever synonymous with integrity.

The Protagonist Wishes to Express the Truth, However Cryptically: A Cryptogram

A	B	C	D	E	F	G	H	I	J	K	L	M	N	O	P	Q	R	S	T	U	V	W	X	Y	Z
6					5				20			14	23				21								

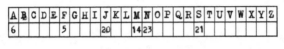

```
                    S   N                     M    S M   F
___ __ __ __ __    __ __  __ __   __ __ __   __ __ __ __  __ __ __
12  1  18 17 18    16 21  23 22   18 7  26   1  18 14 16 21 14  5  22 17

                            M   A
                         __ __ __ __ __ __ __
                         10 7  24 16 14 16 6
```

Full

I snuck off to be alone. I took the car and drove to town as though it called to me, drawn toward secrets, lost in the tide of reason. I bypassed GI, drove right past the familiar—like a wife about to slip into someone else's bed.

Walking through the doorway of the unfamiliar place, I scanned the room for the flash of a familiar face, and, when I did not find one, I slid into a corner table and hid from view. I did not know why I was there. It was as though I had come coerced by the notion of relief.

This diner was Greek too—Greek American restaurants known as a "Coney Island" restaurant, are established and plentiful in Detroit. Coney Island restaurants center around the (absolutely freaking delicious) Coney Island hot dog, which is loaded with chili, diced onions, yellow mustard, and sometimes relish. It is usually referred to simply as a "coney" and named after the similar hot dogs served at the actual Coney Island which was one of the first stops of immigrants after leaving Ellis Island. Greek brothers established coney restaurants in Detroit around 1915, and they have been an establishment in Michigan ever since. With dirtier walls, cheap but delicious fare, and a gray-countenanced wait staff who stank of being, this coney was nothing like GI. The tables were sticky, the air thick and greasy on my cheeks, the walls lined with posters of greatly varying Hellenic achievements—the Parthenon, Sappho,

Zorba, Maria Callas, the Olympics, and—last in the row—Irene Papas as Electra.

Electra—the Argive princess and daughter of King Agamemnon, the father she worships and has lost. She must avenge his death. She cannot live until she has. Electra laments in her grief, *Evil is all around me, evil / is what I am compelled to practice,* Sophocles wrote.[25]

The teenage waitress interrupted my distraction, and I ordered a pathologically healthy omelet—egg whites, spinach, mushrooms, no cheese. No toast, nor any other accoutrement of diner breakfast food.

I waited.

Electra called again, her expression goading me toward viciousness: *In such a state, my friends, one cannot / be moderate and restrained nor pious either.*

The omelet arrived: wet. Sickening. In careful squares, I inhaled it. The first in an oncoming surge of secrets.

Father, father, father! Your perpetual excuse!

I ate.

Well-fed.

Surfeited.

Satisfied.

These are the things that one normally feels after the feeding of a hunger. *I'm full,* you will say. *I am sated.*

No other form of satisfaction can compare to the profundity of a body replete.

But there is another kind of fullness, one replete with nothing but disgust.

One might think that in the wake of all that had been lost, one might feel an emptiness. But that is not the case.

Even an empty stomach is ripe with bile, enzymes, and digestive juices. Ready. Excitable. Impatient to pounce on and devour any new artifact it encounters, absorbing the good and excreting the bad—hot acids pummel the contents of the guts, as detergent pummels grease in a pan, turning it to energy and waste.

---

25 Translation. Anne Carson

So it is with grief.

You lie there empty, but your guts are primed and full to bursting with this acid. It's the same sharp acid you watched dissolve your hands and navel and inner organs, the one that has evaporated you many times over. That acid does not live in your guts alone; it has seeped up into your throat, taking away your voice. It sloshes within you as you move through life, burning away your brain as you dream.

You are so full of the tart and pungent stuff that any further introductions are not merely unwelcome, but impossible. The slightest scrap or sliver or slice of nourishment becomes intolerable.

There lies the paradox: though empty, you are too full. Crowded. Crammed. Bursting with the acids of anger, shame, self-loathing, guilt, and deep, unabating wretchedness.

Food could not be tolerated—too full was I of everything else.

The pent up feelings had to be released, in the most violent, punishing way possible.

And o'er this gloom / No ray of pity, save from only me.

But I was not standing before the house of Agamemnon. I was alone, a body still recovering in the filthy toilet of a diner— fluorescent lights flicking, staring downward at shreds of trampled tissue, face filled with broken blood vessels, eyes shot and soundlessly weeping, taking in an unspeakable sight. But for a moment—and only for a moment—relief.

Living creatures will suffer anything for a morsel of comfort. Isn't that a funny thing? Doesn't that just make you want to convulse at comic truth?

One thing I have learned about comfort: do not dare mistake it for hope.

I purged the omelet.

It was the start of a battle that would rage a decade, like the Trojan War itself.

I would fill and empty over and over again, for years, in secret. I would face my broken blood vessels, I would lose bone density, and fill many teeth. Not until pressed to breaking point, not until forcing a choice between what I loved and what I had come to require to regulate the war within, would I truly heal myself. Just like every war, it would be caricatured, cannibalized, ignored, raged, made commonplace, dehumanized, continuously lost, then ultimately, one day, won.

Star of Wonder, Star of Night

I'd attended Jewish preschool when I was very little, but the overwhelming holiday memory of my childhood is Mom's Christmas. That provides wave after wave of shiny memories—glittering trees, dancing in a pink tutu in the living room with Dad while *The Nutcracker* played on our Sony television set, a sea of gloriously wrapped boxes beneath the tree (Mom was always extraordinarily gifted in that department, Dad extraordinarily handicapped). Christmas morning was nothing short of exhilarating, and then we (OK, *I*) spent the rest of the day in a sugar-induced coma of excitement, collapsed in front of *Frosty the Snowman*, clutching my beautiful bounty.

I remember buying Christmas trees. We'd narrow our choices down, presenting each contestant as if it were a beauty pageant, eventually settling on one and even naming it.

I remember in particular Christmas 1995, watching the very first hairs fall from Dad's head at Christmas Eve dinner at a neighbor's house—so gently and silent. It was stirring, but something we could not speak of in company.

I remember the following year, when he surprised us by coming down the stairway stark-ass naked in his woolen cancer hat singing "NYC" from *Annie* while Mom and I rolled on the floor at the bizarre flippancy of it all.

We Silbers had always liked the holidays. We liked hope. And joy. Comfort and joy.

Not so this year. A bleaker and darker December there had never been before or since. We weren't exactly having one of those Christmases you see in the movies. No angels got their wings, no Grinch's heart exponentially grew. This wasn't even jerky animation *Rudolph*, though that felt a bit closer.

The motherfucking holidays.

It was not only our first holiday without Dad, it was the first holiday after September 11. So many were mourning in addition to ourselves. And still the world churned on; we hummed songs of the season in as throated a voice as we could muster. For now, the planet circled the sun, unrelentingly turning upon its axis, opening itself toward the light—light that could only be felt and seen on the other side of this darkness.

It was becoming clear to us that life had to move forward. The five of us had to move on; we had to make decisions about the future. But we didn't have answers, just a great many questions that led to more questions.

Yet one thing was certain: after the New Year, we would no longer be living together at 1367. As we felt the year itself ending, we also felt life, as we knew it, ebbing away—like a radio station flicking and fading as you drive farther away from the signal on a highway.

We bought our tree.

We did our best.

Indulging in Christmas spirit felt a little like taking a drink from a fire hose. Grey and Lilly returned to their homes, but Kent stayed with us for Christmas. Mom handwrote a note to Santa, which she folded into a tiny ball and left next to a few cookies and some carrots for the reindeer. It simply read: "Dear Santa, Thanks for stopping by. I think we need a little extra help this year."

There were a few gifts—mostly handmade, small. I learned somewhere that there is a corner of the NASA website where you can buy the stars in the sky and have them named after people—a process completed with a certificate that comes in the mail. *As if you can really own a star*, I thought as I clicked the screen, scoffing as I went ahead and did it anyway. I not only bought the star, I bought into the beauty of the idea that no matter where I walked or wandered, I could, at some point, look up and see that star named after my father, burning in the night sky.

We had presents that year, but for so many across this planet, there are no gifts. Hope is all that remains.

That year, it may have been a dim, flickering speck, but we had hope too. As well as 1367, and one another, and a sky full of stars.

Death Therapy

"Your 'death therapy' cured me, you genius!"
—*What About Bob?*

In the beginning, truth be told, it happened all the time.

For many weeks, it happened almost every night. I didn't talk about it back then, I worried that uttering a word about the visitations would make me sound like Hamlet (my second-favorite college drop-out with a dead dad, next to myself). I also worried talking about them would make them stop. I didn't want that. I wanted them to continue forever.

I also didn't know if anyone else in the house was also receiving visitations. I would wonder if the reason why Mom hadn't slept well was because she had been up all night talking with Dad. Or I'd scrutinize Grey's bouts of strong emotion, or the look on Kent's face when he could not decide whether or not he had just heard something rustling downstairs. But eventually it was clear to me that I was alone, nose pressed up against a window that gazed upon another realm. Once again listening just outside another kind of door.

( )

Lilly lay beside me, as she always did when the five of us were all together. I glanced over at Lilly's warm, sleeping body before slipping out of the bed, making my way downstairs to the lower-level living room where Dad had always stayed up late watching news or sports, reading or thinking.

And there he was.

Again.

Silent and very still except for a gentle flicking action of his thumb; the thumb of his left hand would begin inside the other four fingers and he'd flick it out, like striking an imaginary match of inspiration. He always did this when he was thinking deeply, and the speed and frequency of the motion could tell you the exact speed of his flowing thoughts.

He sat there in a chair in front of the television in the middle of the night just as he had done in life. He wore the green velour bathrobe and held the stem of an already-eaten apple as he took his eyes away from the TV—which was *actually* on (I checked time and time again when this happened)—to smile at me.

It had been a month or so since I'd had a visit from Dad. About a month. The visitations were becoming more infrequent.

The first time it happened, I had joked. I had quoted Bill Murray, of course—from *Scrooged*. It's what Bill Murray as Frank Cross says when he first sees the ghost of his dead boss: "No, you are a hallucination brought on by alcohol . . . Russian vodka poisoned by Chernobyl!" I had laughed a little when I said it, probably trying to lighten the mood. Dad had laughed too. Then, we both went quiet. Straddling the netherworld didn't put either of us in the mood to get into a Bill Murray quote battle.

Now, I didn't say anything; I just pulled up a chair beside him. I'd already cottoned on to the Rules: his talking was limited and, if we touched, he would have to go pretty much right away. So we usually just sat there, either watching reruns of films we loved together—*Bob*, of course, *A League of Their Own, Sister Act,* and *Shakespeare in Love*— as well as classic films we'd never watched together—*Casablanca, Gone with the Wind, Gentlemen Prefer Blondes.* Sometimes we just sat in silence together, lost in thought.

I wanted to tell him I loved him. I wanted to tell him I knew that I would never stop loving him.

I wanted him to know that I knew we were just alike. I wanted him to know that we were different.

I wanted to tell him that I understood that life without him was going to be hard. But I wanted him to know that I forgave him for leaving me—not without a father, I would say, though I was undoubtedly disappointed about that, but without a guide.

I wanted to tell him that if I had been his mother, he would have been allowed to play baseball. That I understood all he ever wanted was to be a good son, to be approved of and loved by his father. I wanted to tell him that I understood—that I saw him as a giant among men but still recognized that I knew he had been limited by life. I wanted him to know that I understood he was a man and not a god.

I wanted him to know that I did not think he was a failure. That I understood that no amount of talking, or wrestling, or overreaching logic could ever explain the behavior of his parents, and that desperately striving for their love had been his Achilles's heel, his kryptonite, the weakness that defeated him. I wanted to say that I forgave him part of that responsibility, but not all. *Because you taught me better than that*, I might say.

But I did not say a thing.

I did not have to.

When love is that strong, some things—most things, in fact—do not need to be said to be understood.

We just sat there as we always did, side-by-side, soaking in these moments—moments we had both been robbed of. He reached across the chair and, breaking the Rules, he grabbed my hand and squeezed it tightly—just as he did the night before he died, with a grip so strong, it cannot be described in words. I felt an unspoken love so great no vessel could hold it, save perhaps the vast infinity of the sky.

I woke downstairs in the chair just before dawn—as always—draped in the blue hush of early morning.

Dad was gone, leaving only a distant waft of his cologne and, of course, an apple stem.

Where Memories Go

From the time I was little, I have always clutched fiercely onto ordinary moments. If I shut my eyes tightly and memorized every detail, I could paint and repaint the moment with white-knuckle accuracy and will myself to remember, over and over again. Writing it down felt like cheating, so I would stare and think, contemplate and document with my mind alone as I stored more and more details away, terrified that even *one* might escape me.

But would they be there in twenty years? Would they remain in their place, right where I had left them? Or, like all natural things, would I return to find them turned to dust? Disintegrated by time and neglect? Might I return to the Great Library of Memory to find that entire sections had been destroyed by a fire, or ravaged in a storm, or sold off to another city to pay for modern repairs?

Would I remember the way I wept on my first day of First Grade at El Rodeo School when Tara Pascal told me it was not the first day of fall and called me a liar when I insisted it was? Would I recall how I cried so fervently because my Mom had told me it was the first day of fall, but really it was because I didn't know anyone at my new school and I felt so achingly alone? Or how Mrs. Divine (true to the name) held me and told me it was *indeed*, the first day of fall, and that everything was going to be all right very soon?

Would I remember the taste of a Flintstone's push-up ice cream? The way the cardboard would get soggy, and the way my heart sank when I reached the bottom?

Or would I recall being disheartened when that girl at preschool raced to the dress-up box and got the gold shoes before everyone else?

How about the way my skin stuck to my dad's black leather chair as I spun round and round, accompanied by the hum of his vintage IBM typewriter?

The quality of the California light?

The exquisite awe of my first winter in Michigan?

And the sounds of my father's breaths—his final breaths—through a bedroom door?

What of all those seemingly forgettable everyday moments? The *in-betweens*, the *forgot abouts*, the *oh yeahs*? What of them? Would they one day be precious? Would they one day be treasured vintage volumes?

The thought of losing any of them petrified me.

I wanted them, no matter how unremarkable they were.

Even then, I wanted them all. I still do.

Have you ever wondered where memories go? Do you suppose memories are stored in a kind of great library with a comprehensive card catalog filled with time-worn cards, all dog-eared, fingered, and browned with age that notate the time, and place, and subject of each encounter, each vision, smell, and feeling in alphabetical or chronological orders? Where will your wedding day be logged? What is the exact decimal configuration of learning to read? The ISBN number of the day your heart first broke? Your first taste of chocolate? Your last sight of home?

Prim librarians with pinched mouths would shush you as you ran up and down a long unexplored aisle, children you faintly recognize guide you to sections you thought were long destroyed. These are our guides, and they will sit you down and insist you pore and pore over the pages of newly rediscovered volumes. Or they will point the way toward your favorite titles, reminding you (harshly or gently) that though you may have your favorites, there are millions of unexplored tomes, not to mention a world beyond the library itself. Great collections begging to be explored—the basement of lies, the catacombs of dreams.

And as you collect more and more memories, the aisles and rows of books all magically lengthen. They elongate alongside your experiences with infinitely expanding and elevating shelves, and nothing, not a long-lost garment, an airplane seatmate, or a kid from the playground goes uncataloged. Same for our less than impressive lunches, boring school lectures, the scents of strangers' perfumes, and fathomless snippets we'd prefer to forget. They are all there, in perfect order.

Libraries all have different cataloging systems based on their functions, but one thing is certain—unless it is a collection of academia or a medical library, there is always a children's section. When you pass the section in adulthood your mind wanders back to the days when you belonged there. The sticky smell of spilled food on stuck-together pages; well-worn stories read again and again (and again) by readers you could connect with only by the name scribbled in a child's printing on the front-page card. Illustrations. Little tables for little bodies, reading. There is the children's section and there is everything else.

In years to come, this event would define that border of childhood for me: there was everything before he died, and everything that came beyond it. There is *Before* and there is *After*. Perhaps that is why the librarians employed in this section of my Memory Library take such great care. The titles are precious, they have greater weight for they cannot be shared with, or expanded upon, by him.

Further, every new book will be cataloged, organized, and above all, measured by its relation to the Great Event. This is where library cataloging becomes complex: is the new volume close in proximity to the Great Event, or far—and close by date or close by subject relevance? There will be countless ordinary days, but also anniversaries, Father's Days, birthdays, graduations, opening nights. In years to come, where will these be shelved, these memories from *After?*

I am running in the early morning through Glasgow park with my class-mate Kirsten on October 9, 2002. I have only been in Scotland for three weeks, and it all feels very foreign. Kirsten offers me company, a card and little candies, and is generally so kind to me on that very strange first anni-versary of Dad's death. She makes it special, understood. What it marks is that there shall never be another "first without him" moment ever again.

I am in my second year of drama school in Scotland when I fully realize that every single person I ever meet again will never know my father. It isn't like my mom, who these wonderful people have all heard about and might meet *someday*. I weep at the magnitude of the uncountable friends, lovers, partners, children that shall never know him, and in the midst of this despair, my soulful friend Rebecca Sloyan grips me tightly, insisting that she *does* know him, through me.

I am in London. My close friends Beverley, Tomm, and Julie from the West End production of *Fiddler on the Roof* take me out to celebrate what would be my father's seventieth birthday at The Ivy. I reflect on the gift of being able to finally say a proper goodbye to him in the train platform scene. As my character Hodel declares every night on stage: "Papa, God alone knows when we shall see each other again," her father Tevye responds "Then we shall leave it in His hands . . . " We talk about him. We raise glasses of champagne. It is a magical night.

I am in Edinburgh during out of town previews for the West End pro-duction of *Carousel*. I am learning the nature of what my mother lost through Julie Jordan—what it really means to not merely lose *someone*, but to lose *the only one*. On the seventh anniversary, a two-show Thurs-day, Lesley Garret sang, "You'll Never Walk Alone" straight into my still-aching heart, not once, but twice.

I am opening a birthday card from Damian, the love of my London life. Damian is very good at cards, and remembering dates. The card is handwritten, and addressed to "Mike." It updates him on my life thus far and congratulates him on raising a great kid. Damian promises "Mike" that he'll look out for me. I won't save a lot of things from London, but this one I'll never part with.

I am painting my New York apartment on the eighth anniversary of his death. Mom is here to paint the kitchen a teal-blue named "Mermaid's Dream," and the furniture hasn't arrived yet, so we sleep top-to-tail on an air mattress and make "T-shirt pillows" laughing so hard we nearly forget the date. We light a candle and keep painting.

I am weeping backstage at the Samuel J. Friedman Theatre on Broadway. Weeping uncontrollably after exiting on the opening night of *Master Class*. I have performed this play, with this cast, countless times, but after exiting the stage as Sophie DePalma on the night of my Broadway debut, I weep. For it is in these moments that I always remember he will never be here—that every victory is also about his absence.

I am sitting in the cinema watching Sierra Boggess in the live performance of *Phantom of the Opera* at Royal Albert Hall. As she sings "Wishing You Were Somehow Here Again," I burst into tears for I know so much of our summer sharing a dressing room at the Samuel J. Friedman Theatre was learning about and holding our individual aches. As I turn my phone back on after the ending, I receive a text from her: "*Soph: you were with me tonight and so was your father. That one, was for you.*"

I am being walked down the aisle at the Tony Awards by Danny Burstein, the "Papa" I have come to know in the Broadway production of *Fiddler on the Roof*. I will never be walked down the aisle by my own father, this is the closest I shall ever come, and to do it while fulfilling a lifelong dream, and having the world bear witness to it, is a level of explosive joy so piercing and poignant that as the dancing reaches its peak, I can smell my father's cologne. I cover my face to keep the scent close. I shout, arms raised, exploding with joy.

I am sitting in a hospital bed in midtown Manhattan, being kept overnight for observation. To my left is Lilly, asleep: still my best friend, still looking out for me. At the foot of my bed, I see him. Dad. He is wearing a beautifully tailored black suit, looks happy, at peace, and in the prime of health. With his presence are also warm breezes and bright light. I know this is not a dream. I know I am gazing at the portal but do not yet belong there with him. I rip myself away from it and return. He was right all those years ago: it *is* everything you hope it is and now I do never have to fear it.

❨ ❩

Neuroscientists say every memory is actually the memory of a memory, and every time we remember the same memory, it gets distorted slightly over and over again until at some unnamable point, all we are left with is the skeleton of truth draped in the fabrics of our imagination. I have been told that I have a photographic memory. But after thirty years and change of life, I have really only managed to hold on to what feels like a few measly scraps.

Who are we without our memories? Who are we if we make no meaning of them? Above all, what belongs to us?

What are we meant to keep?

PART FIVE:
TOMORROW

Emma and Her Dad

In June of 2016, after a performance of *Fiddler on the Roof* on Broadway (in which I played the oldest daughter, Tzeitel), I met a young girl at the stage door of the Broadway Theatre. She was accompanied by her father. The two of them were waiting in the crowd that had gathered outside the theater door on Fifty-third Street to get an autograph, to say hello.

The daughter, I eventually learned, was named Emma, and she was beautiful. A young woman of maybe thirteen or fourteen. Her face was punctuated with a bright-red lipstick and trendy glasses, and I was tickled to see that she still had her braces. The lipstick with the braces was charming—a little giveaway of her youth, as was her unabashed excitement at the stage door, and, of course, the presence of her father.

This had been their second time seeing the show, and they appeared to be overcome with feeling. The sight of them immediately lodged a quiver in my throat—one of sentiment and envy.

For me, it was just an ordinary Tuesday. The audience had been lively and responsive, but this wasn't a particularly remarkable night post-show —no glamorous guests or special events. I didn't have any personal friends who had come to see the show, so I was looking forward to heading home and getting to bed in anticipation of a two-show Wednesday. Broadway was amazing, but it had become ordinary life. How quickly had this dream I had had since childhood become quite commonplace, as so many dreams do. That was no bad thing. It is reality, it is life. It does not take away from the sense of honor, gratitude, and service. But eight shows a week is tough, repetitive, physically and emotionally grueling work, no matter how rewarding. We achieve our goals. Our dreams come true. Or they don't. Either way, we must always strive for new dreams.

Emma's father was trying to hide the intensity of his emotions by plunging his hands into his pockets; you could tell he was overwhelmed to be sharing this moment with her. I asked if they did this often.

"We do," he answered, "but honestly we should do it more."

Their faces were raw—this timeless story of fathers and daughters had affected them deeply, and tonight, I had been a part of that story.

God, I loved the theater.

God, I missed my dad.

"Are you an actor?" I asked Emma, and her bright red lips revealed her braces as she smiled broadly. Her dad smiled, too.

"Tell her," he said, nudging her arm.

"I *want* to be," she said, adjusting her glasses. "I—" she hesitated. "I hope to be."

They smiled at each other before looking back to me.

A hand from beyond this world placed itself upon my heart and stopped it for a moment.

It was my dad. He was there, reminding me about the lobby of *Ragtime*.

Emma: fourteen years old, just like I had been. A young girl whose father longed to do "more of this"— just as I know my father longed to make every possible memory with me while we still had time.

I wanted to tell Emma and her father everything. I wanted to tell them to travel, to watch all the movies, to take all the walks, and say all the things. I wanted to tell them to make every memory possible, to make every one count, because we never know when the chance might be taken from us.

But I didn't say any of that. I knew what I was supposed to say. My dad's hand was holding my heart from the other side of the Great Beyond and he was giving me my cue, not that I needed it. It was time to pass the baton. I knew my line.

Emma's face looked up at me: the face of a young actress, standing beside her father, who was looking up at a woman she had just seen perform on Broadway. Emma wanted to act.

"You will," I said, perfectly on cue.

And then I cried. The circle had been completed and my dad was there—I felt him.

Emma and her dad walked away that night, likely not realizing the gift they gave me. As I walked toward the subway on Fifty-fifth Street, I desperately wanted to call my dad up to tell him that I met "us" tonight. That Judy Kaye's prophecy had come true. That I had "done it," and in a manner more meaningful than could ever be imagined.

I couldn't call Dad, but I did the next best thing. I called Judy Kaye.

New Year: The Last Hurrah

Deep in the shadows of old Jerusalem, the ancient Jews fought against oppression. They joined together, rose up, and defeated the oppressors who had outlawed their faith and desecrated their holy temple.

In the ruins of their newly won city, the Jewish people stood in the silence and agreed: they had to cleanse and rededicate the temple. They would reignite the menorah—a beacon of light that would burn all day and all night—as a symbol of their fortitude and their faith.

Olive oil was required to keep the menorah ablaze within the temple. But when the Jews returned to their oil supply, the Talmud says, they found that there was only enough oil to burn for a single day. They would need eight days to prepare a new supply of oil; the light in the temple would be doused long before then.

But a miracle happened. The oil in the temple lasted eight incredible days: exactly the time needed to prepare a fresh supply of oil for the menorah. Thus, Hanukkah, the Festival of Lights came to be.

Beyond all reason or logic, hope—like the light in the ancient temple of Jerusalem—is inextinguishable. In the darkest and most desperate hours, when we mine ourselves for more than we ever could conceive was possible, the fuel for hope is there. So that we may continue on.

Hope may be fragile, but it is there, just like the light.

Sometimes blazing, sometimes merely a tender, trembling flicker that, regardless, cannot be extinguished, that flame winking. So our ancient ancestors have taught us. So we continue to learn again and again as time churns ever onward.

Hope accompanies all new beginnings.

And all new *years*.

On December 21, the winter solstice and darkest day of the year, we hatched a plan to take place ten days later on New Year's Eve to escort us all from 2001 into 2002.

It was the winter solstice, and our corner of the planet may have been at the very furthest distance from the sun, but it was only going to get brighter, bit by painstaking bit, from this point onward. It was on that day that it came to us in a flash: the idea for the Great Party. The most concentrated endeavor we could, or indeed would, ever create together. An idea born, in every way, out of darkness.

We had discussed spending New Year's Eve together previously; we had made some sketchy plans, thought about dinner reservations and the like, but as Kent and I spoke (on two different phones in 1367) with Grey in Madison, Wisconsin, four days before Christmas, the great New Year's Eve plan was born.

"A Great Party!" Grey announced. "Jay Gatsby style . . . "

A Great Party on December 31, we thought, *of F. Scott Fitzgerald proportions.* It would be the only way to cleanse us.

Just like that, it was absolutely settled.

Sometimes we simply must surrender. The act of letting go unleashes a kind of fathomless healing power.

Sometimes, if we are lucky and have our eyes fully open, our minds act like the shutter of a camera—capturing a moment perfectly from the just-right angle in the just-right light.

Sometimes, we just have to trust and practice a little serenity.

And sometimes you just have to pause and say, to heck with all that, it is time for fancy steak. Filet mignon, to be exact (or, as Lilly calls it, "cute meat," taken from the literal French) because that is how this New Year's Eve party was going to roll. Well, actually, that was how Grey rolls, and the rest of us obviously jump on that medium rare bandwagon because cute beef is delicious. There we were with a cute, expensive cut of beef and an even more a-cute hunger.

But you don't just stir-fry that cute meat up with wok veggies! No! *Très mauvais!* Grey marinated our cute meat for two days. You need to infuse. You need to create some irresistible juices. You need to sear that cute meat after stuffing it with an entire clove of garlic. You need to pre-pare a homemade Béarnaise sauce, two starter courses, and three finishers to accompany it. That's right, six courses. Because we could. Because why not go out with a bang?

After all, Great Parties are all about letting go and about creating perfect moments captured in perfect lighting while donning a black tie. There is a whole lot of serenity that comes in the form of champagne and very strong gin and tonics. And steak. Really expensive, delicious steak.

How do you do all of this, you ask? Well, because you know that your friend Grey is excessively cultured, Kent has an (admittedly peculiar) ado-ration of Martha Stewart-like household preparations, Catherine has the finest clothes available in the state out in the garage, Lilly is a musical genius, and you are *driving*.

And because, dammit, we were all crazy like that.

We were desperately crazy.

We liked it that way.

Grey was the undisputed mastermind behind the menu.

"Slice the pears," Grey ordered Lilly.

"What am I, a surgeon?" she said, her perfectly made-up eyebrow a wry question mark.

We were all in black tie (arranged by Mom of course) but Lilly was wearing one of Mom's many *Alice in Wonderland* pinafores as an apron. Mom had fetched theater-themed aprons for all— Dorothy from *Wizard of Oz*, Alice from *Alice in Wonderland*. Everyone wore one, including Kent, who looked positively dashing as Drake from *Annie*.

We had all just completed what we would dub that night as Petit Noel—though there was nothing petit about our Noel, for we went all out purchasing and making gifts for one another in far greater excess than any of us did for our families on real Noel. The living room looked like Santa's North Pole workshop had been blown up in the middle of this suburban Detroit House of Death. This crew wasn't going out with a bang but with a nuclear explosion, and the wrapping-paper massacre in our living room was evidence of that.

Our New Year's Eve version of Petit Noel had exploded beneath our glittering tree and was complete around 9 p.m., far too late to begin cooking despite the pre-preparations already in place for our six-course feast. Pears sautéed in balsamic and butter with Gorgonzola sprinkles were first, and all of us were tending to our various jobs to get ready for the assembly line of tasks ahead.

Mom lit candles and made the salad (there is no better salad maker on earth). Lilly and I assisted Grey with the homemade Béarnaise that would accompany the filet mignon we were now taking out of the marinating bags from the refrigerator, allowing the meat to get to room temperature before it was cooked. We shared oven mitts and sharp knives, moving around one another in the open kitchen in a very tipsy-on-life-at-a-wedding manner as we clinked glasses and stirred sauce.

"I'm playing DJ," Lilly said. "I think it's time for some George and Ira."

"Great idea," agreed Cathy from the living room. She was already vacuuming up Petit Noel in her ball gown, preparing an improvised dance floor.

We poured cocktails as the Gershwins serenaded us from the stereo. The ladies danced in the living room before Grey's shriek called us back to the kitchen.

"Girls!" he cried, "I *need* you! Perfect full-cloves-of-garlic-needing-to-be-inserted-into-the-steak needs you!"

We were on it.

At last the food was perfect, the aprons hung, the table set, the candles lit, and all that remained to be done was to savor every scrap of it before midnight.

The moment hung suspended in the air: the five of us stood around the table and stared at one another, smiling. We had really done it—out-done it, truth be told.

"Boys," Cathy said with a smile, looking to Grey and Kent, who promptly made their way to Cathy's chair, pulled it out and helped sit her down in the gown as if they were experts. They did the same for Lilly and me, then took their own seats themselves.

We lifted our champagne flutes by their stems.

"Here's to us!" Kent said, somehow encompassing everything in those three little words.

"To us!" we said together.

And with that, the feast began.

There was the smoking of cigars (even by my mother) and of "manly pipes" received at Petit Noel, which Grey and Kent puffed away at in their matching corduroy jackets.

There was running around barefoot in the front yard and street. And there were leftover fireworks from some Fourth of July that we had found in the laundry room. There was the throwing of an odd Israeli bottle of wine that Albert and Edna had re-gifted us into the River Rogue behind the house. There was singing (of course) and sidesplitting, migraine-inducing laughter. The music blared from a stereo that lived within the antique Italian bureau in the center of the upstairs living room.

It was a much-needed New Year and new beginning. We were dressed in black tie and 1367 was dressed in magic.

The open presents and dirty dishes lay in neat and not-so-neat piles, respectively. The drinks flowed as freely as our laughter. The air sang— it was all twinkling lights and rich fabrics, glorious music, full voices, champagne bubbles, and a slowly ticking clock, nearer and nearer to the appointed hour.

We felt relieved.

We felt powerful.

We felt like dancing.

So we did.

Then the countdown began. As the clock struck its chimes, the world moved slowly, each second's passing prolonged, as if through water, so one might better see the details of each infinitesimal millionth of a moment.

We would continue to gather in this manner for annual Great Parties at the New Year, for years. Until every last one of us was a grown adult, with jobs and lives scattered to every corner of the planet. Someday all of this would be like a dream—one so clear and real you could just swear it had really happened, only to wake and forget by midmorning.

Every year was a little bit different, but every year was the same—the five of us gathered to celebrate our joys and share our sorrows together.

First, Lilly—faithful Lilly. She will live and love greatly. At the banquet of life, Lilly will return for thirds, having most likely licked her plate. Lilly will end up in Santiago, Chile, as the principle oboist with their National Orchestra. She will visit in every city you shall ever live in and you will travel and work and weep and laugh together. You will share many adventures (such as getting robbed on a night train in Italy, and Lilly teaching you music for your very first West End audition that shall become your professional debut). You will, oddly, never see the house she grew up in. But you will always be one another's number one. No matter if you live across the planet (which you shall) no matter what the high or the low, the glittering success or terrible agony.

Then Grey—glorious Grey, with his tender heart, talent, humor, and white-hot mind. In a few short weeks, Grey shall indeed be in Australia, beginning a new life on the other side of the world. He will become exactly the great and important Broadway designer you all know he is destined to become. You will share long talks well into the night and no one will listen with more attentiveness, nor absorb your own love with more ferocity. One day, you both end up in the very same place, holding one another's hands as you move through your lives and parallel careers.

And of course: Mom. The greatest lover of life you have ever—and shall ever—meet. She will never be the same. But her ability to find joy in the darkest of corners, her optimism, spirit, and genuine joy in life, shall continue to rock you to your core as you grow older. And in the days to come, the collection of days in which all of your own theatrical dreams come true, she will be there to share it—every last scrap of it—with you.

And then Kent. His eyes say it all—he adores you. Your eyes say it in return. You have never felt such love. From where you stand you can smell his musk, and are filled instantaneously with a feeling of wonder. He will stay, for years. And he will hold you and stand by you and you will grow up together. You will give to one another and advance through this crucial time in both of your lives. Forgive yourself. And never forget him. You know it now more than ever: no one could have done it but him.

And me . . .

The clock had struck.

Champagne flowed and, in the distance people, sang "Auld Lang Syne."

So small a moment is the ticking of a clock. One moment goes by. The present is now the past. The moment to follow, and everything, every single moment ahead, the future.

It was many things, but most of all, it was, at last, tomorrow.

The Morning After

O h God," Kent groaned, so hungover he was blind.

"Oh God," replied Grey. "Even my face is curled in the fetal position."

They were nursing feeble bowls of Honey Nut Cheerios, pawing each O into their mouth individually, with the grace and elegance of hungover bears. The boys could not believe how magnificently, blackout drunk they had gotten last night.

Last summer, when we were all working at Interlochen in our various crappy jobs, perhaps these two created a document entitled "The Pact of Inebriation," inciting both of them to remain as drunk (on vintage Riojas) as (il)legally possible throughout July and August. They took it very seriously. Now? Right now they were uncertain if there was any meaningful way to measure hungover-ness on a historical level, but wondered if someone might want to call the *Guinness Book*.

This was the morning of January 1, 2002.

"If I can get more than halfway up those stairs by noon, then today counts as a win," said Grey, the cogs of his usually nimble mind crustily stumbling along, "Good lord, I can't even form a lucid bitchy riposte." They were certain they had drunk more than they ever had in the past, probably more than anyone has, *ever*.

"I did not so much bruise my brain as I smashed the absolute bejeezus out of it," Kent wailed, clutching his head. "Did you dare me to chug a flower vase?"

"No," replied Grey, "you dared yourself. I just watched."

They were one step short of waking face down in a Jacuzzi in Morocco with a bunch of inexplicable bruises, an inch away from a few counts of indecent exposure screwing up their attempts at college reacceptance, one negligible level below having a mysterious tattoo.

"I feel like Helena Bonham Carter looks when she dresses herself," said Grey. He was on the verge of weeping.

Mom, Lilly, and I looked at the boys, arms crossed in amusement. We were tired, but otherwise fine (whatever "fine" means).

It was not until that morning, beholding this carnage that was this disparate collection of people that I realized it: whom we align ourselves with is the paramount consideration of life. We must choose wisely. Despite the hangovers, here were the most uniquely remarkable people I would ever come to know, who saw their friend and her mother through the very worst days of their lives and did it with compassion, dignity, and most remarkably, humor. Kent, Grey, and Lilly would be inextricable from the narrative evermore, no matter where life took us.

So the five of us chuckled to ourselves, handed out aspirins and glasses of water, and got on with our day. Indeed, all our days. One baby step at a time.

Epilogue

I don't know how to begin this coda.

I wasn't even sure if I should write this coda.

Sometimes in life we entertain, other times we share, inform, revel, reflect. And rarely, we risk revealing a crack in the door enclosing the "other things." The things that cannot always be seen, or held in your hand, or observed in words. The *unutterables*. The deeply felt.

The loss of my father—Mike to some, Mikey to others, Papa to me—has been the defining mythology of my entire adult life.

Sometimes my inner ocean still swells about it.

When I think back on that time, I recall that for some of it, I was asleep.

That's alright.

Perhaps that's how it is with pain: it is like hibernation, a chrysalis of sorts forms around us while we heal. Or transform. Or both.

That is not shameful, not weak. It is necessary.

But I have torn away the barriers of that sleep. I am now awake.

After all this time I have come to realize that I, just like every human being, have had many identities and "lives." Yet all of our many identities reside at the same geographical "address," represented somewhat feebly by our physical bodies. Cells turns over, but memories remain.

I think about those moments when I connect with my father in the present, as an adult. I think about his charisma, his star power, his blinding intellect, and vision. I think about all of the things he loved about me, and vice versa, all the things he wanted for me, fought for, in many ways gave his life for.

I think about him.

Grief is a place we all shall visit, a familiar yet foreign land. You sit at the benches in the town square and without warning, the skyline transforms before you, the seat below you shifts, the beverage you are drinking morphs into another. One can never feel at ease there, only become more acclimatized to the nature of the ever-changing place, learn the rules, the language, the customs—to embrace the cold and strange, but be at peace with it. Because you must: in the Land of Grief, it is not only the cushions that alter, you alter too. And often, you don't always notice when you do.

But sometimes there is nothing you can do about pure, unadulterated, weighted, roaring sorrow.

Frankly, I would not blame a soul if they exercised their right to curl up and die—to capitulate to the agony of loss, collapse upon their dreams and live the remainder of their days flying at half-mast. I would never blame those that do. All I know is something within me refused to. Something within me would not allow it. I chose to live.

To *really* live.

That is my father's perpetual gift to me. When we face our greatest fear so early in life, we must take heart: there is nothing left to be afraid of.

Were there days when all I desired was to merely wake up and breathe, to just allow my heart to beat, not truly caring whether it continued?

Yes.

But I chose to live.

And I did not choose it because there didn't seem to be another choice, not because it is what my dad would have wanted. I lived because *I* wanted to.

Ultimately, I found a place deeper than pain; an invisible but palpable place with ground as sturdy and immovable and as glittering as diamonds—to lift up, to surface, to eat at the banquet of the living even when that meant doing so bite by painstaking bite.

I look back at the child I was, the gifted, old soul, yes; but mostly the inexperienced child facing so much, so many grown up troubles on top of the already heavy decisions and changes associated with that time in everyone's life. She was cut off at the knees, for no matter how much we think we know when we are seventeen or eighteen, we are not done being raised.

Are we ever?

I look back at her as if she was someone else and I want to hug her and tell her it will be all right. I want to tell her that she is stronger than she knows, that even though she has no reason to believe that she will ever be happy again, that she *will*. I want to tell her that when she survives this—and she will— she never has to be afraid again.

I would not judge her now as I judged myself then. I would not tell her—because she would scarcely have believed me—that she would soar to the top of every one of her dreams.

I learned in Scotland that sometimes we must "act as if."

I learned in London that life does get better. That it ebbs and flows.

I learned from the people who loved me before and the people I met along the way that love is infinite.

I learned Fear. I learned Shame. And Regret. Endurance, ugliness, and a deeply personal kind of Faith.

I learned that love keeps going.

I learned that holding on to resentment only hurts you. I learned that forgiveness sets *you* free.

I learned Patience, Serenity, Courage, and Gratitude.

I learned all of this, for it is only in the depths of Grief that we truly learn to value Life.

I have had the greatest adventures anyone could ever hope for. I pinch myself almost every day asking myself, "Is this real life?" Does one person truly get to experience *every* kind of dream? The people I have met, the places I've been, the quantity and *quality* of every experience, every opportunity, every travel, conversation, job, every glorious triumph, every accomplishment and celebration and happiness . . .

Reader: I would trade it *all* for Only. One. Thing. But that is not how it works.

And that is what still smarts. And probably always will.

We cannot make such trades, and so, we must accept with all our hearts what *is*, what we cannot change, and do as much as we can with the circumstances we've been handed. Do not wish or pray away the pain—ask for the strength to endure it so that it may be used for further understanding, to view each trial as an opportunity. Before we can rebuild our life, we must come to know the peace that accompanies acceptance, for out of peace arises the willingness and the wisdom to greet each day with the freedom of an open, loving, trusting, and *resilient* heart.

Whoever you are, no matter how despairing or isolated, know this: being fully alive and fully present in all of your experiences—joyful and harrowing—is a human right worth fighting for. We are limited in life only by what we believe we are capable of. I am not remarkable. No. I am a human being just like you—capable of everything from the most deplorable of errors to the vastest glories. As are we all. But I endeavor to show up: to work, to love, to grow, to *life*. No matter what any of it chooses to serve.

When we stare deep into the black infinity, when we truly take part in the democracy of loss and mortality, we recognize that all of us—no matter how wealthy, beautiful, talented, kind, willful, adventurous—die. We all die. You will, someday, die. And in the end, we all must face the same questions:

Was I brave?
Did I use my gifts?
What did I believe in?
What did I stand for?
What did I stand against?

Did I do what truly mattered?

Did I love enough?

It has been said that wisdom is a guide upon which to chart the journey of the spirit.

Wisdom is precious.

And wisdom is earned.

It is not about what happens to us; it is how we choose to respond to life, that matters.

Thank you, Papa.

Thank you, Grief.

Half a lifetime on, I feel stronger and more grateful than ever.

Onwards, with courage and integrity.

Acknowledgments

"I'm sailing!"
—*What About Bob?*

Several close friends lent constant warm hands—not merely creatively but held my hand when the reviewing of such challenging memoires became, at times, unbearable. Bobby Steggert, Tasha Sheridan, Amy Maiden, Elizabeth Stanley, Alexandra Socha, Amy Jo Jackson, Frances Thorburn, Kit Baker, and of course, to Lillian Townsend Copeland. They helped me bear it. These are all the truest of friends who constantly hold me accountable, buoy me, and above all, gave me the courage.

To Sierra Boggess, Tyne Daly, Rabbi Larry Hoffman, and of course, Judy Kaye—for their invaluable gifts of friendship and inspiration. To Samantha Massell and Rachel Sussman for eleventh hour inspiration and support. In addition, thanks is owed to the great Bill Murray, Greek Islands Coney Restaurant, and to Interlochen Center for the Arts.

I am indebted to my first readers of this work: Julia Murney (and her beautiful card sent in the actual mail after completing my first draft), Morgan James (who was so determined a friend to finish reading, she printed out the draft page by page at the front desk of her hotel in Mexico), Stuart Piper (who read this in its infancy from one side of the Atlantic to the other), and Allie Beauregard—my collegiate voice of reason.

My students from Pace University Classes 2016–2018—who held up a mirror of their talent and their youth, reminding me of what it means to be eighteen years old, and taught *me* simply by being themselves. Who showed me that I would never dare to hurt and punish them as I had to hurt and punished myself. You will always be my "Purple Warriors." Particular thanks is owed to Katie Hollenshead—for being the young person I needed to help encourage me to share my truth without shame, and eventually gave me the gift of setting me free.

To my inextinguishable, beautiful mother Catherine. You are grace, joy, depth and resilience. You make Dolly Levi look like a stick in the mud. Thank you for all you've given me and thank you for allowing me to have my own experience with both death and life. You're not only my mother you're my friend. To Rabbi Daniel Syme (the only "character" in both of my as-of-yet published novels). To Roberta Sorvino—without your guidance both I, and this volume, would be a shadow of what it was.

Unending and never-forgotten gratitude to and for Justin Flagg and Dane Laffrey—my saviors, my heroes. To friends Haley DeKorne and Jessica Modrall. To my teacher Judy Chu (who taught me to meaningfully read and write). And to my Interlochen acting teachers and mentors David Montee and Robin Ellis, who nurtured within me every important theatrical truth, and gave me a space to grow into the artist I am today.

To my agent Joelle Delbourgo, my manager Jeff Berger, magical editor Iris Blasi, and to Pegasus Books for all taking endless chances on me.

Crucially, to my wonderful brother Jordan Silber and his beautiful young family—my sister-in-law Maggie, and nieces Hannah, Madison, and Charlotte. Despite having a half-brother seventeen years older than myself, I had the childhood experience of an only child. This chronicle reflects that sentence. We did not grow up together, but in our adulthood I have come to know and love you (along with your beautiful young family) *very much*. Not only to love you—to *like* you! How many families can say that? I recognize that we had very different experiences with our father and our family. I respect your experience utterly, and love you unconditionally—more than words could ever say.

The penultimate debt of gratitude goes to Louise Lamont. Louise, without you, I would not *be* a writer, and *White Hot Grief Parade* (in particular) would not exist. You found, cultivated, nurtured and in many ways partially built the writer I am, and no language could ever express my infinite love and gratitude.

Above all, to my father, my dad, my *Papa*: Michael David Silber. I loved you, I still love you. Thank you. See you soon.

AHOY.

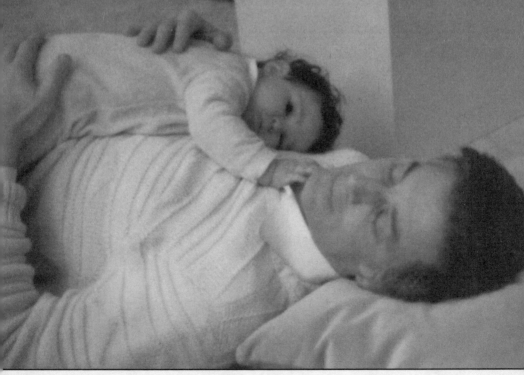

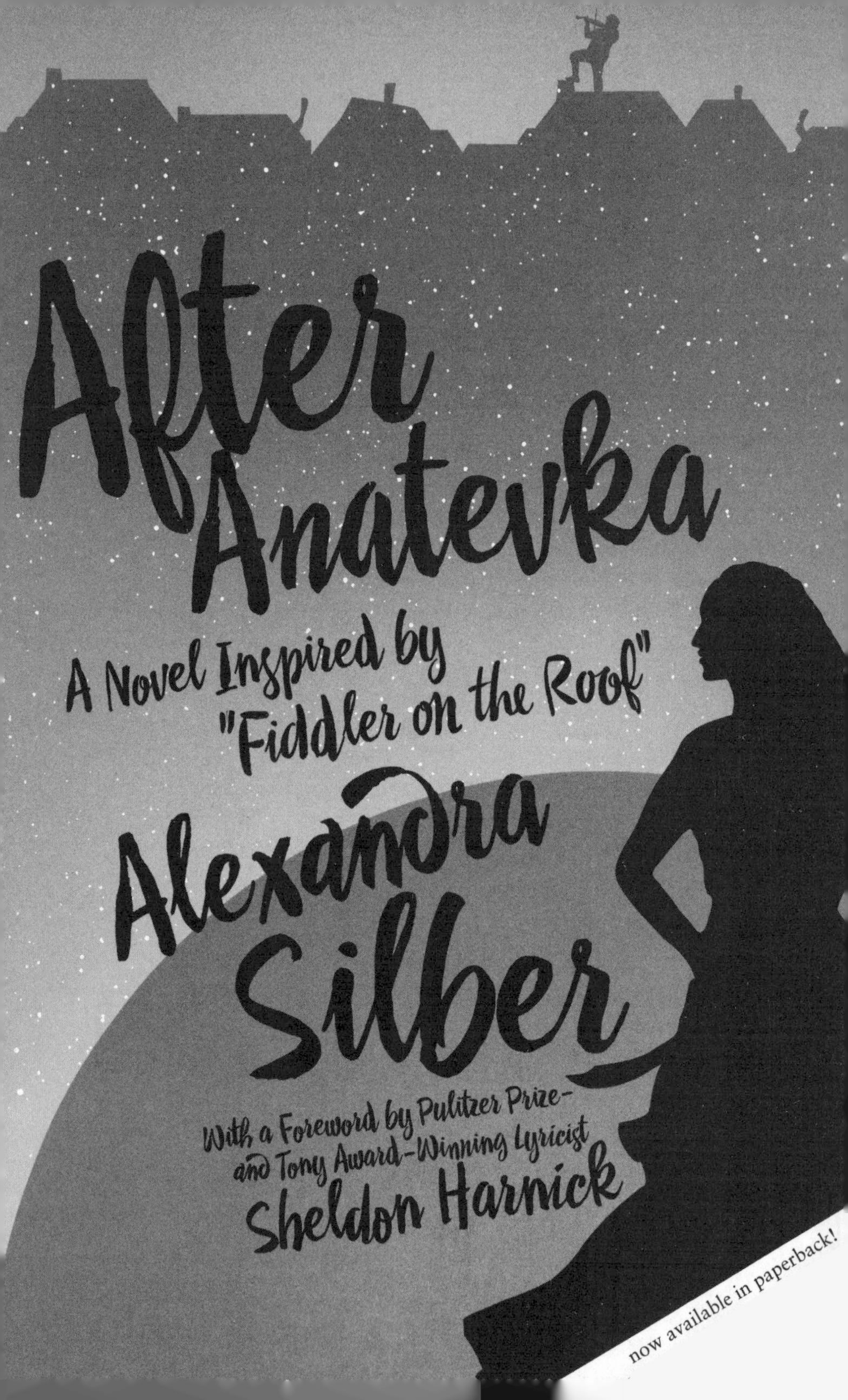
After Anatevka
A Novel Inspired by "Fiddler on the Roof"
Alexandra Silber
With a Foreword by Pulitzer Prize- and Tony Award-Winning Lyricist
Sheldon Harnick
now available in paperback!